D1431363

GAME OF MY LIFE

MINNESOTA

GOPHERS

GAME OF MY LIFE

MINNESOTA

GOPHERS

MEMORABLE STORIES OF GOPHER FOOTBALL

JOEL A. RIPPEL

FOREWORD BY
CHARLIE SANDERS

SPORTS
PUBLISHING

CONTENTS

FOREWORD

I was just a country boy and didn't really play organized sports until junior high. I didn't play football until 10th grade. I never pictured myself having a career as a football player. I didn't play it because I thought I'd play it in college or the pros. I played football because I enjoyed it.

When I was in high school, I wasn't aware of much outside of North Carolina. Playing football at a Big Ten school was the furthest thing from my mind. I thought I'd end up playing basketball at a small college like North Carolina A&T. I played in a high school football all-star game and (Gophers assistant coach) Bob Bossons saw me. The first I heard that Minnesota was interested in me was after that game.

I decided to visit Minnesota. I knew (Gophers basketball All-American) Lou Hudson. We had played basketball together. It was nice to know someone at the University when I visited there. Visiting Minnesota was such an eye-opener for me. Coming from the racial tensions of the South in those days, Minnesota was so ahead of the South and what life could be like for a black man trying to fit in. The visit was so positive that I didn't visit anywhere else.

When I got there, I played four positions in four years. The coaching staff was so great. Coach (Butch) Nash. Coach Bossons. Coach (Murray) Warmath. They cared about us as human beings. The more you got to know Coach Warmath, the closer you got to him. He was such a caring individual. I had so much respect for him. He was like my father, he didn't say much, but he didn't have to. When you got in trouble on or off the field. He would just give a look that demanded respect—nothing else needed to be said.

When I got the news (that I had been elected to the Pro Football Hall of Fame), Murray was one of the first people I called. I wanted to let him know how much I appreciated everything he had done for me. I can't say enough good things about him.

Hearing about this book brought back great memories for me. The 1967 team (my senior season, when the Gophers were Big Ten co-champions) was so talented, and it was a very close-knit group. I think we had 10 or 11 guys off that team drafted.

What I remember most about the University was, it was the best place for me. It made me more open-minded in getting along with people. I remember the brotherhood of my teammates—guys like (Gordon) Condo and (Thomas) Sakal. I couldn't have gotten a more valuable education than the one I got at Minnesota.

I've been blessed. I played football because it was fun; and I was rewarded tremendously.

Through the years, I stayed in touch with former teammates. I know you'll enjoy this book.

—CHARLIE SANDERS

ACKNOWLEDGMENTS

I would like to thank Mike Pearson, who presented me with the opportunity to work on this project. I would also like to thank Travis Moran of Sports Publishing LLC for his patience.

I'd like to thank Niels Aaboe and Julie Ganz of Skyhorse Publishing for the opportunity to work on this second edition.

I'm grateful to several of my *Minneapolis Star Tribune* colleagues— Mark Craig, Chip Scoggins, and Sid Hartman—who were helpful in tracking down former Gophers. Dennis Brackin and Patrick Reusse of the *Minneapolis Star Tribune* shared their knowledge of Gopher football history and made very helpful suggestions.

"M" Club President George Adzick, an All-Big Ten safety in 1976, was a big help in locating former Gophers.

Alicia Jerome, Stacy Bengs, Paul Rovnak, and Jeff Keiser of the University of Minnesota Athletic Media Relations office were a tremendous help with pictures.

Finally, I'd like to thank all of the former Gophers, who took the time to be interviewed for this book.

INTRODUCTION

Even though I grew up in Southern Minnesota, just 130 miles from the Minneapolis-St. Paul Metropolitan area, a trip to the "Cities" was rare for me.

One of my earliest memories of a trip to the Twin Cities is with a church group for a Gophers football game. While I don't remember many of the details of the game other than the score (a 35-35 tie) and the opponent (Ohio University), I do remember vividly being in awe of the crowd and the atmosphere at Memorial Stadium. I instantly became a fan of college football.

Working on this project has made me realize how much of a college football fan I still am.

Legendary Minneapolis newspaperman Sid Hartman, who has covered University of Minnesota football for more than 60 years, has said that for much of the first 70 years of the 20th Century, Gophers football was the biggest thing on the Minnesota sports scene. Reading game accounts via microfilm of the *Minneapolis Star*, *Minneapolis Tribune*, *Chicago Tribune*, and *Los Angeles Times* allowed me to understand how big Gophers football really was.

I think we've managed to put together an impressive lineup of former Gophers who have recalled many of the big Gophers games of the last 70 years. It's too bad that we no longer have the opportunity to talk to former Gopher greats like Bruce Smith, Paul Giel, Leo Nomellini, Bob Hobert, and Sandy Stephens and former coaches Cal Stoll and Butch Nash about their memories.

Because Gophers football has provided Minnesotans with so many great rivalries, great memories—six national championships with 20 former Gophers coaches or players in the College Football Hall of Fame—I'm excited that this book about Gophers football is being published in the fall of 2007, the 125th anniversary of the first Gophers football game.

Editor's Note:

Since the book was first published in 2007, some of the circumstances surrounding the players featured have changed. Though we've worked to preserve the original text and added chapters on Ed Lechner and Eric Decker, please note the following:

• Sonny Franck passed away in 2011 at the age of 92.
• Murray Warmath died in 2011. He was 98.

Chapter 1

SONNY FRANCK

EARLY LIFE OF SONNY FRANCK

Laura Franck was so elated when she gave birth to a son, she called the newborn "Sonny."

"My mother had a boy (several years earlier), and he died. So, she wanted a boy badly," Franck said. "(When I was born), I was her 'Sonny Boy.' She kept calling me her Sonny Boy; and after two months or so, she dropped the 'boy' and just called me 'Sonny.' A county recorder came around and said, 'Laura, you have got to name this boy.' So, she named me George, after George Bendix, the doctor who brought me into the world."

Growing up in Davenport, Iowa, Franck was a multiple-sport athlete.

In the fall, there was football. In the winter, there was basketball. In the spring, there was baseball and track.

"The St. Louis Cardinals were interested in me," said Franck. "I was a good hitter with a level swing. My dad didn't want me to play pro baseball. I was a lousy basketball player, and the football coach (at Davenport Central) wanted you out for track."

Franck was a natural at track.

"A guy named George Champion was living in Davenport," said Franck. "He said to me, 'You've got a lot of natural speed. You'd be a good halfback.'"

NAME: George "Sonny" Franck
BORN: September 23, 1918
POSITION: Running back/
   defensive back/punter
HEIGHT: 6-0
WEIGHT: 176
YEARS: 1938-1940
ACCOMPLISHMENTS: Two-time
   all-conference selection (1939,
   1940); consensus All-American
   (1940); elected to College
   Football Hall of Fame (2002).
GAME: vs. Iowa—October 26,
   1940

Others noticed Franck's speed as well.

"The University of Iowa wanted me to run track," said Franck, who ran the 100-yard dash in 9.6 seconds and the 220 in 21.1 seconds. "They didn't want me to play football. I wanted to play football."

Champion told a friend in Davenport about Franck. That friend told an acquaintance in Minneapolis about him. The Minneapolis man told (assistant University of Minnesota coach) Bert Baston, who told (Gophers coach) Bernie Bierman.

"Bierman didn't talk to anyone for more than five minutes, but my dad was just like him—a hardheaded German," said Franck. "They sat in Bierman's office for two hours. On the way home my dad said, 'That's the coach you want to play for.'"

So Franck ended up at the University of Minnesota in the fall of 1937.

"Bierman (who had been at Minnesota since 1932) had never had a fast guy," said Franck. "Nobody knew how to use speed back then."

Under Bierman, who had coached Tulane to a 36-10-2 record in five seasons and led the Green Wave to the 1932 Rose Bowl, the Gophers won national titles in 1934, 1935 and 1936 and a Big Ten title in 1937.

George "Sonny" Franck, a consensus All-America selection in 1940, was the last of the 14 consensus All-Americans from that year to be named to the College Football Hall of Fame.

"In 1937, I was ready to quit," Franck said. "Of the 74 guys on the team, only four didn't play a down, and I was one of them. I was going to quit. They didn't call it red-shirting back then (freshmen were ineligible). One of my teammates explained to me that I would not play in games or go on trips. He said, 'Didn't anybody tell you this?' I said, 'No, this is the first I've ever heard of it. But I used the year to learn the halfback position.'"

During Franck's sophomore season (1938), the Gophers won another Big Ten title. The 1938 championship came despite losses to Northwestern and Notre Dame, which prompted Chicago sportswriter Marvin McCarthy to write of "the disintegration of the dynasty."

The Gophers went through a rebuilding year in 1939. The highlight of the season was a 20-10 victory over No. 10 Michigan in Ann Arbor. The victory moved the Gophers, who were just 2-3-1 at the time, into the Associated Press Top 20 at No. 20. The following Saturday, the Gophers lost to the unranked Hawkeyes in Iowa City, 13-9. The Gophers concluded the 3-4-1 season—their first losing season since 1930—with a 23-6 victory over Wisconsin.

SETTING

The Gophers went into the 1940 season with a lot of talent (three future College Football Hall of Famers—Franck, future Heisman Trophy winner Bruce Smith, and Dick Wildung) and question marks. Observers wondered how the Gophers would respond to their first losing season under Bierman.

In Bierman's single-wing, one-platoon football, Franck, who had been an end in high school, was expected to be versatile. He ran, passed, caught passes, punted, returned kicks, and played defense.

Teammate Bill Daley said, "We were all fast in that backfield, but Sonny was really fast. We would run sprints at the end of practice. By the time he had gone three or four steps, he was at full speed and out of reach."

The unranked Gophers opened the season with victories over two solid opponents—Washington and Nebraska. In the victory over Washington, Franck returned a kickoff 98 yards for a touchdown and made a crucial tackle late in the game—knocking a Huskies runner out of bounds after a long run. The two victories earned the Gophers the No. 7 spot in the Top 25. The Gophers then had two weeks to prepare for their third game (at Ohio State).

"The team wanted to have that Saturday (before the Ohio State game) off to go hunting. Bierman wanted to practice," said Franck. "The team asked me to ask him for the day off, and I said, 'I'm not the captain.' But I went to him, and I said, 'I know we're going to practice on Saturday.' He said we were thinking about pleasure and not football, that we didn't know how important the Ohio State game was. I said, 'We're going to beat Ohio State. I guarantee it. Practice early, that's all I'm asking.' He agreed."

The Gophers outlasted the No. 15 Buckeyes, 13-7, to improve to 3-0.

"We were leading 13-7, and Ohio State had the ball late in the game," said Franck, "and (Don) Scott ran around left end. I took off from the middle of the field and tried to cut him off. I threw everything I had at him and knocked him out of bounds inside the 1, with less than two minutes to play. And, we got the ball back."

The Gophers then manufactured what Franck described as "... the best drive we've ever had. OSU had been holding us. We needed two first downs, and we got them and went right down the field."

The Gophers defeated the Buckeyes despite being outgained, 384-229. The Gophers, who didn't attempt a pass, rushed for 229 yards. Ohio State completed 11 of 23 passes for 104 yards and had a 16-9 edge in first downs.

Next up for the Gophers was rival Iowa. The Gophers were looking to avenge a 13-9 loss to the Hawkeyes the previous season. In that game, Iowa, which was coming off a 7-6 upset victory over Notre Dame the previous week, scored 13 points in the fourth quarter to rally for a 13-9 victory over the Gophers.

THE GAME OF MY LIFE

BY SONNY FRANCK

Bierman was a tough taskmaster and very low key. When he was angry, he would never blow up, but he would get very sarcastic. He would lower the boom on you, but he would never raise his voice.

During practice the week of the Iowa game, Bierman said, "I know you're an Iowa boy," and he accused me of throwing the Iowa game the year before. I had scored a touchdown in the third quarter to make it 9-0, but Iowa came back. With just seconds left in the game, Nile Kinnick stepped in front of me at midfield and intercepted Harold Van Every's pass to end the game. Bierman accusing me of throwing the game really got me hot under the collar. I was an Iowa boy and knew a lot of Iowa players. Everybody on the team knew how mad I was. The team was all for me. I kicked the ground and vowed I'd get even.

It was homecoming, and there were nearly 63,000 fans—including nearly 10,000 from Iowa, including my parents and brother—in the stands.

Iowa scored first after recovering a fumble at our 33-yard line in the first quarter. Bill Green, my former high school classmate, ran 27 yards for a touchdown to give Iowa a 6-0 lead.

We fumbled the ball away three times in the first half, but we finally got going in the second quarter. I scored on 29- and 44-yard passes from Bruce Smith—about three minutes apart—and we led 14-6 at halftime. We hadn't tried a pass in the previous seven quarters before those two, but we threw eight passes that day. We completed just those two touchdown passes. We didn't throw the ball much all season. In fact, we only passed for 229 yards in eight games that season.

Sonny Franck ran the 100-yard dash in 9.6 seconds and used his speed to win the 60-yard championship at the 1941 Big Ten indoor track meet.

In the third quarter, I returned a punt to the Iowa 36. We drove to the one, where I scored my third touchdown. I carried the ball eight straight times on that drive.

I scored my fourth touchdown on the first play of the fourth quarter, which made it 27-6. Then to boot, Bierman took me out. Back then the rules were you could only sub once a quarter, so I was done for the game. I could have broken Red Grange's Big Ten single-game scoring record.

We ended up winning, 34-6.

Iowa coach Eddie Anderson said after the game that those two quick scores were the biggest factor in the win. Iowa seemed to lose its enthusiasm after the second touchdown.

Football is a team game, and any back is only as good as his line.

My teammates always thought I was a self-centered S.O.B. and cocky. I probably was. But when I was calling signals, I didn't always call my name. I did what was best for the team.

I said after the game that I had to get four touchdowns. My brother Harry got three playing for Davenport high (the night before). I had to beat that.

GAME RESULTS

Franck finished with 43 yards rushing and 74 yards receiving as the Gophers outgained the Hawkeyes, 367-170.

Minneapolis Sunday Tribune reporter Bob Beebe wrote, "He (Franck) took care of his two Iowa pals on his two touchdown passes. The first he snatched over the head of Bill Green with Bob Bender in on the play. The second he grabbed as it sailed over Bender's noggin."

Green said the Gophers surprised the Hawkeyes.

"Last year we beat the Gophers because they didn't have a passing game," Green told the *Minneapolis Tribune*. "We didn't think they had one this year either, until I watched Sonny take those long passes from Smith for the first two touchdowns."

Bierman told the *Minneapolis Sunday Tribune*:

We were pretty wobbly in the first quarter but the boys went to work after that. In the second half they improved on their form of the Ohio State game. They weren't really consistent today, but on the whole they continued their game-by-game development. Yes, it was fun to see those two passes from Bruce Smith to Franck connect, to beat Iowa the way they beat us. Bruce certainly hung those two passes out there for George. He didn't play much more than 10 minutes but he certainly did his job while he was in there. Franck had himself a pretty good day.

The week after the Iowa victory, the Gophers defeated Northwestern, which had beaten the Gophers the previous two seasons, 13-12, to improve to 5-0.

"During the week before the Northwestern game, the newspapers were saying that the Iowa game had been a showcase for me and were calling me a triple-threat," said Franck. "I remember I botched one play in practice and Bierman said, 'Well, you're a triple-threat all right—stumble, fumble, and fall.'"

The following week, the Gophers defeated Michigan, 7-6.

"We were trailing 6-0 when we intercepted a pass in the end zone," said Franck. "So we got the ball at our own 20-yard line. I told Bruce (Smith), 'Nothing's going right. Switch halfbacks with me. So Bruce got the ball instead of me. The defense was confused and four guys grabbed me, and Boo (Smith's nickname) ran untouched 80 yards for a touchdown, and we won 7-6."

The Gophers closed out an unbeaten season with victories over Purdue (33-6) and Wisconsin (22-13). The Gophers' 8-0 season—with five victories decided by six points or fewer—earned them the national title. It was their fourth national title in seven seasons.

Following the 1940 season, Franck, a consensus All-American, finished third in the Heisman Trophy voting behind Michigan halfback Tom Harmon and Texas A&M fullback John Kimbrough.

In early 1941, Franck used his speed to win the Big Ten Indoor 60-yard dash championship (in 6.3 seconds).

In August of 1941, Franck was voted the MVP of the college team that played the NFL defending-champion Chicago Bears in the All-Star game. Franck was selected over teammates Tom Harmon and Jackie Robinson.

WHAT HAPPENED TO SONNY FRANCK?

Franck was selected in the first round (the sixth player taken overall) of the NFL draft by the New York Giants.

As a rookie in 1941, Franck helped the Giants win the Eastern Division and reach the NFL championship game, where they lost to the Chicago Bears, 37-9. Franck scored the Giants' lone touchdown.

Franck spent the next three years in the military, where he reached the rank of captain and earned nine battle stars, seeing action in both the Pacific (Iwo Jima) and Europe (D-Day).

As an air observer, Franck was assigned to the U.S. 4th Marine Division to improve air-ground coordinations. He also flew at least 17 missions as a fighter pilot. In June of 1944, Franck was shot down eight miles offshore in the Marshall Islands in the Pacific. He drifted within a quarter of a mile of the Japanese-held island of Wotze before he was rescued by a destroyer's whaling boat.

Following World War II, Franck played three more seasons with the New York Giants before retiring and going to work briefly for Standard Oil. After that, Franck became a high school teacher and coach. Franck spent 30 years at Rock Island (Illinois) High School.

In 2003, Franck was enshrined to the College Football Hall of Fame. At the age of 85, Franck played in the annual Hall of Fame flag football game.

Franck was the last of the 14 consensus All-Americans from 1940 to be enshrined in the Hall of Fame.

"I didn't think I'd get into the Hall of Fame after so many years," Franck told the *Minneapolis Star Tribune* upon his election in December of 2002. "They got a rule that you have to have graduated in the last 50 years to get in. I guess they didn't add it up right."

College football historian John Gunn had campaigned to get Franck inducted.

"John made it all happen," said Franck. "He kept pushing me hard. He didn't give up."

Chapter 2

BILL DALEY

EARLY LIFE OF BILL DALEY

Growing up in a small farming town during the Depression, it was a challenge sometimes for Bill Daley to find an outlet for his interest in sports.

"We played everything, football, baseball, basketball," said Daley. "But it was tough to find enough kids to play, because a lot of the kids were farm kids and they were always needed to help out in the fields."

Daley, whose father was a railroad engineer who worked out of nearby St. Cloud, developed into one of the top athletes in Melrose, Minnesota, and Melrose High School managed to field a pretty good football team. Daley helped the Dutchmen compile a 12-1-1 record in his junior and senior seasons. As a senior, Daley was recognized by the Minnesota State High School League as one of the top players in the state.

Daley developed a goal of playing football for the University of Minnesota and coach Bernie Bierman.

"I listened to Gopher games on the radio," said Daley, who was the oldest of four siblings. "They were the national champions in 1934, 1935 and 1936. In 1934, when I was 15, I went to see a game (in Minneapolis). I sat in the end zone for 25 cents and saw the Gophers beat Chicago, 35-7. It thrilled me so much—the band, the

NAME: William E. Daley
BORN: September 16, 1919
POSITION: Fullback/defensive back
HEIGHT: 6-2
WEIGHT: 215
YEARS: 1940-1942
ACCOMPLISHMENTS: First team All-Big Ten (1941); All-American (at Michigan) in 1943.
GAME: at Michigan—October 25, 1941

whole atmosphere. I saw my hero—Pug Lund."

But Daley initially delayed his dream of playing for the Gophers to pursue another interest. One of Daley's uncles—his father had grown up in Milwaukee as one of 17 children of Irish immigrants—had introduced the young Daley to another sport.

"I had taken up boxing when I was in grade school," said Daley. "During one summer, I visited an uncle in Chicago, who was a boxer. I worked out with him and he showed me the ropes. I went back to Melrose and told Coach Baumgartner that I wanted to start a boxing team. We boxed against St. John's and Sauk Centre. So, after high school, I wanted to be a professional boxer. I moved to Chicago and I started working out at a gym. But I was told DePaul was looking for football players. I found I (was good enough) to play (college football) but then they dropped football.

"I was told to write (University of Minnesota track coach) Jim Kelly, who was an assistant to Bierman and he told me to come," said Daley. "I met with Bernie (Bierman), and when I saw him it was like seeing the second coming. I had always wanted to play for the Gophers."

SETTING

Daley finally arrived on campus as a freshman in 1940. Daley joined a team that was coming off a 3-4-1 record in 1939—the

---

In 1940, the Gophers backfield included three future pro football players—Bill Daley (shown here), Bruce Smith, and Sonny Franck.

program's first losing season since 1930—and that was, in typical Bierman fashion, deep at the running back position.

Led by great running backs like George "Sonny" Franck and Bruce Smith, the Gophers set out to prove that their record in 1939 was a fluke.

The Gophers opened the 1940 season with a 19-14 victory at home over Washington. Nebraska, the Gophers' second opponent, went into its game against Minnesota intent on stopping Franck and Smith. Daley and William Johnson stepped in to combine for nearly 300 yards rushing in the Gophers' 13-7 victory over the Cornhuskers.

The Gophers rolled through the six-game conference schedule undefeated as they went 8-0 to claim their fourth national championship in seven seasons.

Daley gained 278 yards rushing (fourth-best on the team). The 278 yards came in just 41 carries as Daley averaged a team-high 6.8 yards per carry.

George Barton, whose career as a sportswriter in Minneapolis and St. Paul spanned the first six decades of the 20th century, described that season in his autobiography, which was published in 1958.

"The 1940 football season must go down in Minnesota gridiron history as one of the most successful and thrilling ever experienced," Barton wrote.

The Gophers were ranked No. 1 in the first Associated Press poll of 1941. The Gophers opened the season with victories over Washington (14-6), Illinois (34-6), and Pittsburgh (39-0).

In the victory over Washington in Seattle, Daley and Smith combined for 189 of the Gophers' 213 rushing yards. Two weeks later, Daley got the Gophers off to a good start against Illinois when he raced 72 yards on a fullback opener in the game's first minute.

With the three victories, the Gophers took 12-game winning streak (dating to the last game of the 1938 season) into the showdown with Michigan in Ann Arbor.

The Gophers had a seven-game winning streak in the rivalry—outscoring the Wolverines 173-25 in the seven games—but the 1941

Wolverines were No. 3 (Texas was ranked No. 2) going into the game. The Wolverines had defeated No. 5 Northwestern, 14-7, the previous week to improve to 4-0 and move up three spots in the poll.

The Wolverines, who were 7-1 in 1940, had expected 1941 to be a rebuilding year (after the graduation of Heisman Trophy winner Tom Harmon), but many college football observers consider the 1941 Michigan team better than its predecessor. The Wolverines opened the 1941 season with victories over Michigan State (19-7), Iowa (6-0) and Pittsburgh (40-0).

For the Gopher game, Michigan added a few end zone seats to make room for the largest crowd in school history (85,700).

GAME OF MY LIFE

BY BILL DALEY

It was a beautiful day in Ann Arbor. A near-perfect fall day for college football. It was the mid-50s with a slight breeze. I was so impressed by the crowd and the (Michigan) band, which marched up and down the field and back.

I was thrilled to be there, even though I was playing for Minnesota, because it was such a beautiful day.

(Bruce) Smith got hurt on our way to the victory. It probably was one of the best offensive and defensive games—the best complete game—I played. I was thrilled.

Bernie (Bierman) was never big on pep talks. We all knew it was Michigan. He didn't have to do anything to fire us up. He worked us hard during the week. Most of the coaching was done by the assistants. He was the manager.

After a scoreless first quarter, we scored late in the second quarter. We got the ball at midfield after a punt. What set up our field position was a great punt by Smith. He had pinned Michigan down at their 12-yard line with a 69-yard punt. They ended up having to punt it right back to us. Bruce (Smith) completed a 43-yard pass to Herman Frickey, which gave us a first down at the Michigan 5-yard line.

On the next play, Smith got hurt and had to leave the game. He didn't play the rest of the game. Two plays later, Frickey scored on a two-yard plunge.

After the touchdown, I kicked off to Michigan's Bobby Westfall on the 4-yard line. He returned it to the 47-yard line and almost broke it for a touchdown. On their first play, they gained two yards on a run and then they completed a 31-yard pass for a first down at our 20-yard line. Westfall got a first down at our 5-yard line, but on second down he fumbled and Bob Sweiger recovered at our 11-yard line.

I carried three straight plays, gaining 11 yards, as we ran out the clock to take a 7-6 lead into the locker room at halftime.

In the second half, we got conservative on offense without Smith, who didn't return, and our defense really did the job. Michigan only threatened twice—once in each half and we intercepted two passes in the fourth quarter. We ended up forcing four Michigan turnovers and we held on for the win. Bill Garnaas intercepted two passes—one in the end zone and one at the 12-yard line—and I intercepted a pass.

(Tackle) Dick Wildung was outstanding for us and it was one of the best games he played as a Gopher.

Most of us who played football were imbued by a sense of achievement. Magnificent things happened during my college football career, but it was one of the greatest games. It was a beautiful day.

GAME RESULTS

The *Minneapolis Star-Journal* reported that Daley went into the game with a sore toe and a charley horse. Despite the injuries, Daley played the entire 60 minutes and finished with 50 hard-fought rushing yards in 19 carries to go with his interception on defense in the Gophers' 7-0 victory—their eighth consecutive over the Wolverines.

Minneapolis Star-Journal sports editor Charles Johnson wrote, "Bill Daley was out there for 60 minutes with a painful foot injury, but he stayed in there and pitched in a remarkable manner. Minnesota's defense was never more alert with Bill Garnaas and Daley."

One Michigan player told the *Minneapolis Star-Journal*, "I thought that Daley was supposed to be hurt. I'd hate to meet up with that guy when he was healthy."

Bierman told the *Minneapolis Star-Journal*, "Swieger and Daley gave two remarkable performances."

Longtime *Des Moines Register* sports editor Sec Taylor wrote, "Daley played the entire game in a grand style."

Former Michigan coach Fielding Yost, who coached the Wolverines for 25 seasons, told the *Star Journal*, "That Minnesota team, the way it played against Michigan, is the best Minnesota team, I ever saw opposed to us."

It was the only loss of the season for the Wolverines (6-1-1).

After the Michigan game, Daley was leading the conference in yards per carry (6.6 yards per carry in 36 attempts).

The Gophers followed up the victory over Michigan with a one-point victory over Northwestern. In week six, the Gophers shut out nonconference foe Nebraska (9-0) before closing out their second consecutive unblemished 8-0 season with victories over Iowa (34-13)—highlighted by Daley's three first-half touchdowns—and Wisconsin (41-6).

The Gophers, who gave up more than seven points just once and gave up just 38 points all season, earned their second consecutive national title—their fifth in eight seasons.

The perfect season improved the Gophers' record to 63-12-5 in 10 seasons (36-8-5 in the Big Ten) under Bierman. Despite the national championship, the Gophers did not play in a bowl game (there were only four bowl games—Cotton, Orange, Rose and Sugar—following the 1941 season).

Daley finished the season with a team-high 685 yards rushing and a team-high nine touchdowns. Daley, who was seventh in the nation in rushing, and Wildung were named All-America. Daley and Wildung had helped the Gophers rush for an average of 257.8 yards per game—third-best in the nation.

Smith, who battled injuries all season, was third on the team in rushing (431 yards) and passed for 320 yards. Following the season, Smith was named the Heisman Trophy winner—the only University of Minnesota player to win the award. Notre Dame quarterback Angelo Bertelli was the runner-up in the Heisman voting.

As a junior in 1942, Daley replaced Smith as the Gophers' left halfback. Bierman had enlisted in January and George Hauser was coaching the Gophers. In the Gophers' season-opening 50-7 victory over Pittsburgh, Daley rushed for 128 yards and four touchdowns. It was the Gophers' 18th consecutive victory. The winning streak came to an end the next week in a 7-6 loss to the Iowa Seahawks, who were coached by Bierman.

Three weeks later, the Gophers rallied to defeat Michigan, 16-14. It was the Gophers' ninth consecutive victory in the Little Brown Jug game. Trailing, 7-0, the Gophers tied it on a 44-yard touchdown run by Daley. Daley finished the game with 77 yards in 12 carries. The Gophers finished the 1942 season with a 5-4 record.

WHAT HAPPENED TO BILL DALEY?

Following the 1942 season, Daley enlisted in the Navy, and in 1943 Daley was stationed near the University of Michigan campus. When Michigan coach Fritz Crisler, who had coached the Gophers for two years in the early 1930s, heard about Daley being nearby, he asked Daley if he wanted to work out with the Wolverines.

"I told him I had three years at Minnesota and I had enough of playing football," said Daley.

But Daley ended up playing for Michigan in 1943—earning consensus All-America honors. With Daley and Elroy "Crazy Legs" Hirsch (who had played for Wisconsin the previous year) in the lineup, the Wolverines ended their nine-game losing streak to the Gophers with a 49-6 victory. Hirsch scored three touchdowns and Daley scored two touchdowns as the Wolverines handed the Gophers their worst defeat in 22 years (since Michigan defeated the Gophers, 38-0, in 1921). The victory—the most lopsided in the 34-year history of the Little Brown Jug to that point—meant Daley was never on the losing side in a Little Brown Jug game.

Daley was a first-round selection by the Pittsburgh Steelers in the 1943 draft. Before starting his pro career, Daley served as a naval officer in the South Pacific. Following World War II, Daley played three seasons in the All-America Football Conference before retiring from football. Following his retirement from football, Daley worked in radio and for Josten's.

But Daley had a dream.

"I always wanted to be an artist," said Daley. "But I didn't have the talent or the time. I started collecting pinups—pulp art. I remember Pug Lund asking me, 'What does a football player know about art?' I was so lucky. Illustration art made me a rich man."

Chapter 3

BUD GRANT

EARLY LIFE OF BUD GRANT

At the age of eight, Bud Grant was diagnosed with polio. The virus left his left calf and thigh smaller than his right. Despite the diagnosis, Grant's doctor encouraged him to continue playing sports.

"In those days, there were no antibiotics. If you had tuberculosis, you went to a sanitarium. If you had polio, you were supposed to have bed rest and special massages and baths," Grant told the *Minneapolis Star Tribune* years later. "He (Dr. Simcock) told my parents (Harold Sr. and Bernice) not to pamper me. He told them to get a bicycle and baseball mitt and encourage me to be athletic."

Sports became a big part of Grant's life.

When he wasn't playing whatever was in season, Grant, who was the oldest of three sons, worked odd jobs to make money to help his family. His father's salary as a Superior city fireman didn't go far during the Depression.

In 1939, at the age of 12, he worked in his father's concession stand when the New York Giants held training camp in Superior.

"My mother called me Bud, but my dad always called me 'The Kid,'" Grant said in his Pro Football Hall of Fame induction speech in 1994. "He'd tell Giants coach Steve Owen: 'The Kid will play for you someday.'"

NAME: Harold Peter Grant
BORN: May 20, 1927
POSITION: End-defensive end
HEIGHT: 6-3
WEIGHT: 199
YEARS: 1946-1949
ACCOMPLISHMENTS: First team
    All-Big Ten (1948, 1949);
    CFL Hall of Fame (1983); Pro
    Football Hall of Fame (1994).
GAME: vs. Ohio State—October
    15, 1949

Despite having to wear lifts in his left shoe, Grant developed into a three-sport star at Superior Central High School.

About a month after graduation from high school in 1945, Grant enlisted in the U.S. Navy. Grant was sent to Great Lakes Naval Station just north of Chicago.

"My whole adolescence was based around becoming prepared to go and save the country," Grant told the *Minneapolis Star Tribune*. "The fellows I played ball with went to war, and some didn't come back."

Grant was shipped to a base in San Francisco where his unit prepared for an invasion of Japan. In August of 1945, the war with Japan ended. The unit returned to Great Lakes Naval Station, which had a football team coached by Paul Brown and Weeb Ewbanks. On December 1, 1945, the base team defeated Notre Dame, which was ranked No. 5 after being ranked as high as No. 2 earlier in the season, 39-7.

After the war ended, anyone in the service who was enrolled in a college and still stateside could get an early discharge. Grant enrolled in the University of Wisconsin and was discharged.

But by the time he got home to Superior, he changed his mind and decided, that after being away from home, he wanted to be closer to home. He enrolled at the University of Minnesota.

"I had lost my wanderlust," said Grant. "Minneapolis was 200 miles closer to Superior than Madison was. Wisconsin (coached by

Bud Grant, who earned nine letters in three sports at the University of Minnesota, was named Minnesota's athlete of the half century in 1950.

Harry Stuhldreher, one of Notre Dame's legendary Four Horsemen) offered me $100 per month, a part-time job and the use of a car as long as I kept my grades up. (Gophers coach) Bernie Bierman offered nothing. I liked that."

SETTING

In post-World War II, Bierman began building the Gophers into the powerhouse they were before the war. The influx of veterans like Grant and running back Billy Bye, who had been teammates on the Great Lakes Naval Station team, and athletes like Clayton Tonnemaker and Leo Nomellini gave Bierman a solid nucleus to build around.

The Gophers went 5-4 in 1946 and then opened the 1947 season with a 7-6 victory—Grant scored the only touchdown on a fumble return—over Washington in the mud and rain. The Gophers went 6-3 in 1947.

The 1948 season saw the Gophers improve to 7-2. The only losses were a three-point loss to No. 7 Northwestern (19-16, after the Gophers led 16-0) and a 27-14 loss to top-ranked Michigan. Northwestern would go to the Rose Bowl later that season while Michigan, the defending national champion, went on to repeat as national champion.

The Gophers closed out the 1948 season with four consecutive victories—Indiana (30-7), Purdue (34-7), Iowa (28-21) and Wisconsin (16-0). Grant, who primarily played defense in 1948, was named All-Big Ten following the season. The strong finish gave the Gophers, who led the nation in offense in 1948, reason to be optimistic heading into 1949.

From the start there were high expectations for the 1949 Gophers. The headline on a story in the *Chicago Tribune*, previewing the Gophers' season, said: "Gophers aim to win Big 10, Rose Bowl. Buckeyes bar Pasadena way."

Partially fueling the Rose Bowl dreams was that Michigan and Northwestern were ineligible for the Rose Bowl because of the Rose Bowl's contract terms with the conference.

The Gophers opened the 1949 season with a 48-20 victory over Washington and future Pro Football Hall of Famer Hugh McElhenny, who returned the opening kickoff for a touchdown. Victories over Nebraska (28-6) and Northwestern (21-7) improved the Gophers to 3-0 and moved them to No. 5 in the Associated Press poll heading into the showdown with No. 11 Ohio State in Columbus.

The Buckeyes, who had been 6-3 in 1948, had opened the season with victories over Missouri (35-34) and Indiana (46-7). In week three, the Buckeyes tied USC, 13-13.

The Buckeyes, who boasted three running backs who had been high school state sprint champions, had one flaw—fumbles. The Buckeyes had fumbled six times against Indiana and seven times against USC.

Fueling the anticipation for the game was that the Gophers and Buckeyes hadn't played in the previous two seasons. The Buckeyes had won the previous three meetings between the two—39-9 in 1946, 20-7 in 1945 and 34-14 in 1944. The last Gophers victory in the series was 13-7 in their 1940 national championship season (the teams didn't play between 1941-43).

After practice two days before the game, the Gophers boarded a 6:30 p.m train for the 700-mile trip to Dayton, Ohio. After arrival in Dayton on Friday, the Gophers worked out at the University of Dayton and spent Friday night in Dayton before traveling the final 75 miles to Columbus on Saturday morning.

It was clearly the most important game for both teams in almost a decade, and the game caught the attention of the national media. Newspapers played up the Gophers size vs. Buckeyes speed angle with headlines like: "Gophers send 3½ tons of brawn vs. Buckeyes," "Gargantuan Gophers loom large," and "Fesler hopes to stop goon-sized Gophers."

The game even brought out celebrities: Bob Hope, Miss America, Miss Minnesota, and Miss Ohio were all in attendance.

GAME OF MY LIFE

BY BUD GRANT

In 1948, we had become contenders, but we weren't aware at all, at least I wasn't, of the expectations for our team.

I spent all summer in Northern Wisconsin and didn't come to Minneapolis until the day before we started practice. In fact, I had to pass a correspondence course just to be eligible, so I wasn't aware of much of the hoopla.

Bernie (Bierman) was an old-school guy. He didn't like the fact that I didn't play spring football because I was playing baseball. I wasn't on scholarship, so he couldn't punish me. At the start of practice every fall, I was listed on the fourth team. It wouldn't be until the first game that he would move me up. That was just his way of showing the rest of the team.

Back in those days, there was no television. There weren't a lot of football magazines. The magazine racks at newsstands weren't full of football magazines like they are today. I think there was only two football publications—one of them was *Street and Smith's*.

So we didn't know how good Michigan was. Or who was good on Ohio State. I didn't have great aspirations of the Rose Bowl. In other words, football was part of my life, but not all-important. Some guys today, all they think about is pro football. I didn't think I was going to get drafted in the first round.

So, going into that game, it was business as usual for us.

I think that kind of talk (size vs. speed) was probably more prevalent in that part of the country—Ohio, Michigan, and Pennsylvania. College football was so big in that part of the country that the media got swept up (in the hype). In Minnesota, we didn't get swept up in all of the talk that much. I don't think many of us saw those newspaper headlines. Bernie wasn't the kind of coach to post them in the locker room. I've been in places where the coach did.

The train ride there was pretty low key. It's not like we could sit up and play cards all night. Bernie didn't preach to us, but he told us to get in at certain times. We just got into our berths. Coaches were up and down the aisles. It was nothing like the troop trains I was on while in the service. There was no frivolity. There were no harmonicas.

The day of the game was warm. We wore those old wool uniforms. You really worked up a sweat in those.

I enjoyed playing defense. I'd rather play defense because as an end in our offense, there wasn't much to do because we didn't throw the ball much.

In our defense, we did the same thing all the time. We didn't blitz, we didn't stunt. But I do remember making a play early in the game. I was playing defense and they ran a draw play and I got a clear shot at the ball carrier. I had a good run at him and got a clean shot. I tackled him for a loss and he had to leave the game. We were able to make a couple of big stops in the first half.

In the second half, our running backs—Billy Bye and Dick Gregory—really played well.

In the single wing, which we ran exclusively, the tailback had to be a runner and a passer. Billy, might have been a better defensive player than offensive player. He had small hands, but he was able to recognize defenses. We didn't pass the ball much that day but he completed a couple of big passes for us.

Gregory was a good player. He was a good runner. He was a track star and fast. He had a big game.

I was able to catch a couple of passes in the second half. In our offense, we didn't have many (pass) patterns. It didn't leave much to the individual.

That was a pretty good team we beat. We had a lot of talented guys and a lot of good personalities.

GAME RESULTS

The Gophers overpowered the Buckeyes, 27-0, before 82,111 (the third largest crowd in Ohio Stadium history) by withstanding two threats by the Buckeyes in the first half and then breaking the game open with two touchdowns in a two-minute span in the fourth quarter.

Trailing 7-0, the Buckeyes drove to the Gophers' 4-yard line where the drive was stopped by a fourth-down incompletion. Late in the first half, trailing 14-0, the Buckeyes reached the Gophers' 15. On fourth down, Grant and Art Edling dumped Jerry Krall for a 14-yard loss as time expired.

Grant, who had caught just three passes in the Gophers' first three games, had a reception that set up each of the Gophers' fourth-quarter touchdowns. He made a 14-yard reception to give the Gophers the ball at the Buckeyes' 20. On the next play, Bye threw a 20-yard touchdown pass to Jim Malosky to put the Gophers up 20-0. Less than two minutes later, after recovering a Buckeyes' fumble, the Gophers had a fourth down at the Buckeyes' 10. Grant caught an 8-yard pass for a first down at the 2. Don Beiersdorf scored on the next play.

The Gophers limited the fleet Buckeyes, who had scored 94 points in their first three games, to 10 first downs and 48 yards rushing. The Gophers rushed for 284 yards as they outgained the Buckeyes, 339-231.

Gregory rushed for 129 yards, and Bye, who hadn't been expected to play much, rushed for 77 yards and completed four passes for 47 yards and a touchdown.

"Keith Stolen was the star of the game for us," Grant was quoted in the next day's *Minneapolis Sunday Tribune*. "When we lagged in the second half, Keith made 75 percent of the tackles and stopped Ohio from scoring. He was more responsible for victory than anyone."

Dick Anonsen of the Gophers told the *Minneapolis Sunday Tribune*, "Ohio was down on our 5-yard and I'm getting an ulcer. Bud Grant looks at me and winks. What a (cool) guy."

The victory installed the Gophers as the favorite for the Big Ten title and the Rose Bowl berth. The national media was impressed. A headline in the *Minneapolis Sunday Tribune* said, "Visiting scribes hold this opinion: Rose Bowl Bid virtually sure."

The following week, Bierman worked the team hard in practice because he didn't want a letdown. Bierman, hoping to avoid a repeat of the previous week when the Gophers were late arriving at Ohio Stadium, had the Gophers arrive at Michigan Stadium four hours before the game. Later that day, the Wolverines upset the Gophers, 14-7.

Bierman worked the team even harder the next week leading up to the Gophers' homecoming game against Purdue. The Gophers were a 26-point favorite and the Boilermakers brought a 1-4 record into the game but Purdue stunned the Gophers, 13-7.

The Gophers regrouped to win their final three games, but the back-to-back losses cost them the Big Ten title and a trip to the Rose Bowl. The victory over Ohio State was the high point of the post-World War II portion of Bierman's 16 seasons as Gophers coach.

The 1949 Gophers had three players selected in the first round of the NFL draft. The three—Grant, Nomellini and Tonnemaker—were future Hall of Famers. Teammate Gordy Soltau was a third-round pick as 13 Gophers were selected in the draft

The Gophers went 1-7-1 in 1950—Bierman's last season as coach.

WHAT HAPPENED TO BUD GRANT?

Following the 1949 football season, Grant decided to forego his senior basketball season and signed with the Minneapolis Lakers.

Grant, who had earned nine letters in three sports at Minnesota and was voted the Minnesota athlete of the half-century, elected to play two seasons for the Lakers before signing with the NFL's Philadelphia Eagles for the 1951 season.

As a rookie in 1951, he played defensive end. In 1952, he switched to offense and was second in the NFL in receptions (56) and receiving yards (997). Following the season, he asked for a $9,000 contract for the 1953 season. When the Eagles offered only $8,000 he turned it down and signed to play for the Winnipeg Blue Bombers of the CFL (for $10,000). He led the CFL in receptions in three of the next four seasons.

In 1957, at the age of 29, he became the coach of the Blue Bombers. In 10 seasons, Grant led the Blue Bombers to 102 victories and the playoffs eight times. The Blue Bombers made it to the CFL championship game six times—winning it four times.

In 1967, Grant became the second coach of the Minnesota Vikings when he replaced Norm Van Brocklin. The Vikings reached the playoffs in Grant's second season and over the next 10 years were one of the most successful teams in the league. The Vikings reached the Super Bowl four times during that time.

In Grant's 18 seasons as the Vikings' coach, the Vikings won 12 division titles. After retiring from coaching, Grant remained as a consultant to the team.

Grant was elected to the CFL Hall of Fame in 1983 and the Pro Football Hall of Fame in 1994.

"I was never fired, never cut," Grant told the *Minneapolis Star Tribune* in 1994. "I lived where I wanted to. I have benefited more than most people from sports."

Chapter 4

BOB McNAMARA

EARLY LIFE OF BOB McNAMARA

Only one thing occurred in Bob McNamara's hometown on Saturday afternoons in the fall while he was growing up.

"Listening to Gopher football on the radio," said McNamara. "That's the only thing that happened in our small town."

McNamara was a big fan of coach Bernie Bierman's Gophers.

"When I was young, I followed the Gophers," said McNamara. "That was during the Bruce Smith era. Guys like Bill Daley and Sonny Franck were my heroes. Then the 1949 team with Leo Nomellini, Clayton Tonnemaker, Gordy Soltau, and Bud Grant—they were four years ahead of me at the University—they were my heroes too.

McNamara was one of six sons raised by Eva McNamara (his parents were separated). McNamara's mom was worried that her sons would get hurt while playing football.

Bob McNamra's oldest brother (Don) didn't play football, but the second oldest (Jim) did. Jim McNamara was able to convince his mother that it would be okay for the younger brothers to play football. It's a good thing for Gopher fans that Mrs. McNamara let her sons play football—Bob and his younger brother Dick (Pinky)—would go on to play for the Gophers.

NAME: Robert John McNamara
BORN: August 12, 1931
POSITION: End/halfback/
   linebacker
HEIGHT: 6 0
WEIGHT: 190
YEARS: 1951-1954
ACCOMPLISHMENTS: First team
   All-America in 1954; First team
   All-Big Ten in 1952 and 1954.
GAME: vs. Iowa—November 13,
   1954

"My mother worked nights at the Hastings state hospital," said Bob McNamara. "She worked 10 p.m. to 7 a.m. She was amazing. We really respected her. And, we had our influence of our coaches. Fortunately we listened to them about staying home and staying out of trouble. My mom became a big football fan. I think she saw more football games than anybody I know, and she also saw a lot of basketball games."

After earning All-State honors as an end as a Hastings high school senior, Bob McNamara's Gophers career was delayed twice.

"There wasn't a lot of recruiting back then, and my brother Jim thought I would be better off going to St. Thomas," said McNamara. "I was a Catholic kid, so I thought that was okay. But I was only there a month or so. I went to my teachers and I told them I didn't think I was ready for this. Then I told a little white lie and said I was going into the service.

"A buddy of mine—Kermit Klefsaas—was at the U and I was convinced to go there. I was on the freshman team, coached by Butch Nash. We had Paul Giel on the freshman team and we scrimmaged the varsity a couple of times. But the next thing I knew my National Guard division had been activated. According to both schools, because of the short time I had been at each place, I officially hadn't been to either school."

McNamara was on active duty for a year before he was able to return to the University.

Bob McNamara was an All-America running back in 1954 after leading the Gophers in receiving as an end in 1953.

"When I got back, freshmen were eligible and I had the G.I. bill to play for school. I couldn't have planned it better than the way it worked out," said McNamara.

THE SETTING

Bernie Bierman was replaced as the Gophers coach following the 1950 season.

New coach Wes Fesler built his offense around Giel, who would be a two-time All-American and was the runner-up in the Heisman Trophy voting in 1953.

But the Gophers won just 10 games in three seasons under Fesler—prompting another coaching change.

The Gophers went into the 1954 season with a new coach—Murray Warmath—and low expectations.

"If you're a competitor, you're apprehensive about any new coach. Murray was a Southern guy so we didn't know much about him. When he first got here, Warmath called us all together," said McNamara. "He said, 'We have two options. The first is, if the seniors want to play they'll have to work hard. If not, we'll switch to the younger guys.' At spring practice the seniors said, 'We didn't come here to take a dive as seniors.' We were good competitors. We wanted to prove to Coach Warmath we could compete. During spring practice we proved it, and he stuck with us. I admire him more than any coach I've had. With Murray it was simple—if you didn't practice hard, you didn't play. I like that kind of coach."

In the preseason Big Ten poll, the Gophers were picked to finish last. One Minneapolis newspaper predicted the Gophers would win just three games in 1954. The Gophers exceeded those lowly expectations in the season's first four weeks.

McNamara, who had been moved to running back for his senior season after leading the Gophers in receiving in 1953 as an end, played a big role in the turnaround. McNamara shared the backfield with his brother Pinky, making them the first set of brothers to play in the same backfield for the Gophers since Babe and Jack Loomis in 1895.

In the season-opener against Nebraska, The Gophers were trailing 7-6 in the third quarter when McNamara scored on a 3-yard run. The Gophers never trailed again in their 19-7 victory.

The next week against Pittsburgh, the Gophers only led by six (13-7) at halftime before McNamara started a productive second half with a 65-yard punt return for a touchdown. The Gophers went on to win, 46-7.

The following week against Northwestern, the Gophers trailed 7-6 in the second quarter before McNamara scored on a 33-yard run. The Gophers went on to win 26-7 to improve to 3-0.

In the Gophers' 19-6 victory over Illinois the next week, McNamara scored the game's first touchdown on a three-yard run, set up the Gophers' third touchdown with a 33-yard reception and made a crucial one-handed interception to stop an Illinois threat. For those efforts McNamara was named "Midwest Back of the Week," by one of the national wire services.

The 4-0 start moved the Gophers into the No. 8 spot in the Associated Press Top 25 poll, but the following Saturday Gophers lost to Michigan, 34-0, in Ann Arbor.

The Gophers rebounded to defeat Michigan State, and Oregon State to improve to 6-1.

The Gophers, now ranked No. 13, were set to face the No. 9 Iowa Hawkeyes at Memorial Stadium.

GAME OF MY LIFE

BY BOB McNAMARA

I had plenty of things to give me incentive against the Hawkeyes.

Iowa and Minnesota is a great rivalry. Back then it was probably even a better rivalry. We had been pretty average the previous three seasons. We had only beaten Iowa once (with one tie) in the previous four meetings.

In 1953, in Iowa City, we got our butt kicked. Playing in Iowa City was tough enough with the fans right on top of the bench, Paul

(Giel) had carried the ball 14 times for just 13 yards and passed for just 22 yards. I had gotten a concussion. We got beat 27-0 and got outgained 370-81.

Iowa was a good team. Real solid. They had guys like Calvin Jones (a two-time All-American), who was a heckuva ballplayer.

I got goose bumps running onto the field before the game. I was the captain and supposed to be the leader. The night before the game, I couldn't sleep. I'd replay every play we were going to use.

We scored on the second or third play of the game, but Iowa came right back and tied the score.

On the ensuing kickoff, I took the ball at our own 11. I remember getting whacked a couple of times, and I remember Earl Smith jumped on my back. I was struggling and he (eventually) flew off me and the next thing I knew I was out to the sidelines with Jim Soltau and Pink (Pinky McNamara) blocking for me. Jerry Reichow was the last Iowa guy between me and the goal line. I knew Reichow wasn't stopping me. Even if he didn't get blocked, I knew I could make a move on him. Pink wiped him out and I scored, and we were back in the lead.

We knew we couldn't make mistakes and we knew we had to cut them off at the pass. I was playing linebacker on defense.

We never trailed in the game. We were moving the ball a little, but they were moving the ball big time. But we never felt like we were just hanging on. We led by six at halftime.

At halftime, Murray was very realistic about what was going on, like he always was. He had a list of things we could do better. I liked him because he didn't give you a lot of b.s. He told you what you needed to know and always had the big picture in mind.

Late in the third quarter the score was tied again. It looked like Iowa had taken the lead when Smith returned a punt 89 yards for a touchdown. But Iowa was called for holding on the play and the ball was brought back to Iowa's 3-yard line. On the first play, they were

---

In 1954, Bob McNamara (shown here) and his brother Dick were the first brothers to play in the same Gophers backfield in 59 years.

penalized again for offsides and the ball was put on the 1. On third down, Reichow pitched the ball to Eddie Vincent and he fumbled the ball. I almost recovered it for a touchdown, but Vincent was able to fall on it in the end zone and we got a safety.

The last two and a half minutes of the game were crazy.

Pink recovered a fumble at our 16, but the crazy part was on the second play we fumbled it right back to them. They had the ball back at our 18 with about 30 seconds to go. Reichow threw the ball into the end zone, and Shorty Cochran batted the ball away from the Iowa receiver, and Don Swanson, who had just lost the fumble, intercepted a pass in the end zone for us.

In those last two-plus minutes, I kept thinking we had worked our butts off and I couldn't believe we were going to lose the game. I just concentrated on breaking down each play and doing my job as linebacker. I was happy to see them throw the interception. I can still see everything about that game. My wife kids me about it.

Coach Warmath was the happiest I had ever seen him. He told us, "You just played the greatest game I've ever seen."

As elated as we were, we had a sort of letdown after the game. Our quarterback, Geno Cappelletti, had dislocated his elbow in the third quarter and missed the rest of the game. We won the game, but our chances of winning the next week at Wisconsin were hurt. As much fun as we had in beating Iowa, we were in tears over Geno.

GAME RESULTS

Chicago Tribune reporter Edward Prell wrote in his game account, "Minnesota never trailed in a spectacular battle which had even the hardened press box denizens mentally woozy from the opening kickoff."

McNamara's heroics had helped the Gophers outlast the Hawkeyes. The Hawkeyes outgained the Gophers, 398-207, and had a 19-8 edge in first downs in front of a crowd of 65,429. The second-largest crowd in Memorial Stadium history included an estimated 12,000 Iowa fans.

McNamara's 36-yard touchdown run on the Gophers' first drive gave Minnesota a 6-0 lead. His 89-yard kickoff return for a touchdown, which made it 13-7, is considered by many longtime Gophers football observers as one of the most memorable plays in Memorial Stadium history. He intercepted a pass and returned it 22 yards later in the first half.

At halftime, McNamara had 98 yards rushing. With the Gophers leading by two points early in the fourth quarter McNamara recovered a fumble to stop an Iowa drive.

McNamara finished with 226 all-purpose yards (209 in the first half), two touchdowns, an interception, and a fumble recovery in one of the most electrifying performances in Gopher history.

McNamara finished with 115 yards rushing as the Gophers improved to 7-1 overall and 4-1 in the Big Ten going into the regular-season finale at Wisconsin.

Two days after the victory over Iowa, McNamara told the *Minnesota Tribune*, "(In 1953) Paul (Giel) carried the load, he was our team. When he graduated everybody thought the roof would fall in. This was a challenge to the rest of us. We knew we had to work harder without Paul or we'd have a hard time.

"We were picked for the bottom when the season started. The seniors were tired of losing, they made a vow to go all out to win. We knew we had to beat Nebraska to get a good start and we did. It became easier each week to win. Everybody (has) worked hard, and it's paid off. I've never been as happy as I was Saturday after the win over Iowa."

A victory over the No. 17 Badgers, who were 4-2 in the conference, and a loss by Michigan to conference-leading Ohio State, would have given the Gophers second place in the Big Ten standings.

But the Badgers dominated the Gophers, playing without Cappelletti, 27-0, to drop the Gophers into fourth place. The Badgers intercepted six passes.

McNamara finished the season with 708 yards rushing (in 112 attempts) and 10 receptions for 193 yards. He was fifth in the nation in punt returns—averaging 18 yards per return on 14 returns. Following the season, McNamara was named a first team All-

America—the 20th in school history—and was 10th in the Heisman Trophy voting (Wisconsin's Alan Ameche was the winner).

WHAT HAPPENED TO BOB McNAMARA?

Following his Gophers career, McNamara, who had been drafted by the Cleveland Browns of the NFL, elected to play for Winnipeg of the CFL.

McNamara spent four seasons in Winnipeg. For the first two seasons, former Gopher Bud Grant was a teammate of McNamara. Grant then became the Blue Bombers' coach.

McNamara didn't play football in 1959 because of a knee injury. He returned to pro football by playing two seasons for the Denver Broncos of the AFL.

"I could have stayed with Denver," said McNamara. "I had made $11,000 my second season there and they offered $12,000 for the next season. But I had a bar business, which I had started in 1957, and I decided to come home and try out for the Vikings. I thought it was going to be good for business, if I played for the Vikings. I was 31 trying out for the Vikings. I had had four knee operations. I was with them during the exhibition season and then I got released. But it worked out okay."

McNamara's bar, which he had started with Geno Cappelletti, remained in the same location (at Central and University Avenues in Minneapolis) for 47 years.

McNamara, who remains active playing racquetball and tennis, has stayed close to University of Minnesota by helping raise funds for the athletic department and for the new Gophers football stadium. In 2002, he helped direct a $2.7 million campaign that saved the school's golf programs and men's gymnastics team from elimination.

Chapter 5

FRANK YOUSO

EARLY LIFE OF FRANK YOUSO

Frank Youso's hometown is known for two things—cold winters and Bronko Nagurski.

Growing up in the border town in the 1940s and 1950s, Youso had first-hand knowledge of the legendary Nagurski, a former Gopher who is the only player in college football history to be named first team All-America at two positions in the same season and is a member of both the College and Pro Football Halls of Fame.

"We were pretty aware of his legend," said Youso. "But we didn't see Bronko a lot. He was traveling a lot, but we knew a lot of stories about him. When he was around, he was real quiet. He wasn't too quick to talk about football or wrestling. He loved to talk about hunting and fishing and his cabin on Lake Kabetogama. Maybe because he was always in the limelight, he liked the quieter times."

A reminder of Nagurski's stature in the community was the nickname for International Falls High School's athletic teams—the Broncos.

Youso developed into a three-sport standout for the Broncos. Youso's father, like many in the area, worked at the giant paper mill in town, didn't have much time for sports, but supported his son's athletic endeavors.

NAME: Frank Youso
BORN: July 5, 1936
POSITION: Tackle
HEIGHT: 6-4
WEIGHT: 257
YEARS: 1955-1957
ACCOMPLISHMENTS: Second
    team All-America (1957).
GAME: vs. Michigan—October
    27, 1956

"He liked sports, even though he hadn't played much when he was younger," said Youso. "He always said he would have been more interested when he was younger but he was busy working."

Youso played football, basketball, and baseball for the Broncos.

"I did fairly well in basketball," said Youso. "I played forward. We had a pretty big center."

In football, as a teammate of Bronko Nagurski Jr., Youso was named to the *Minneapolis Tribune*'s All-State team as a senior in 1953. Youso decided to play football for the University of Minnesota.

"I had a lot of offers," said Youso. "But a couple of local people took me to a game at the U. Wes Fesler was the coach and Paul Giel was the star. We met Paul after the game. I took a liking to the campus and decided that was where I wanted to go."

Before Youso arrived on campus as a freshman in the fall of 1954, there was a coaching change. Murray Warmath had replaced Wes Fesler as coach.

"We had 285 out for freshman football in the fall of 1954," said Youso. "I remember we were all wearing green jerseys. It was quite a crew. I remember thinking, 'How do you make this team?' But they got us down to 30 to 40 guys and I was fortunate to be one of them."

While Youso worked out with the freshman team, the Gophers went 7-2 in Warmath's first season.

In the fall of 1954, Frank Youso was one of the 285 who tried out for the Gophers freshman football team.

Youso saw his first varsity action in 1955. The Gophers won just one of their first five games—two of the losses were one-point losses—en route to a 3-6 season.

SETTING

The 1955 season did provide one of the most memorable games in Memorial Stadium history. On October 29, the Gophers played host to USC on homecoming. The Trojans, who had played in the Rose Bowl the previous season, and their highly touted running back Jon Arnett were expected to beat the 1-4 Gophers.

But the Gophers pulled out a 25-19 victory in a game the *Minneapolis Tribune* said was played in "perhaps the worst weather ever for a Gopher home game." The conditions—34 degrees, wind, snow and sleet—got worse as the game went on.

"I remember one play," Youso said. "Arnett took a kickoff and was cutting back and forth all over the field. I had three chances at him and I kept missing him. The third time I slipped in the snow and fell near the sideline and Murray yelled at me, 'Get up, he'll be back.'"

Expectations weren't very high for the Gophers, heading into the 1956 season, partly because the Gophers had lost to a team of alumni, 38-24, in the annual spring game at the end of spring practice on May 19.

If the team did have any strengths, one was expected to be the line, with Youso at tackle.

But the Gophers opened the season with a 34-14 victory over Washington in Seattle. The Huskies, in their only season under future Texas coach Darrell Royal, had opened their season a week earlier with a 53-21 victory over Idaho.

The Gophers returned home to face Purdue the following week. The Gophers improved to 2-0 with a 21-14 victory over the Boilermakers and senior quarterback Len Dawson. The victory earned the Gophers the No. 17 spot in the Associated Press Top 20.

The following week, the Gophers and Northwestern, in its first season under coach Ara Parseghian, played to a 0-0 tie on a day that began under warm temperatures and sunny skies but finished in heavy rains. The Gophers couldn't overcome four turnovers as they fell out of the poll.

The following week, Illinois, who had beaten the Gophers, 21-13, the previous season and whose lineup featured two future Pro Football Hall of Fame members—Ray Nitschke and Bobby Mitchell—came to town. Dick Borstad's late field goal lifted the Gophers to a 16-13 victory.

Having survived the Illini to improve to remain unbeaten (3-0-1), the Gophers turned their attention to No. 5 Michigan.

The Wolverines had defeated the Gophers the previous two seasons—34-0 in Ann Arbor in 1954 and 14-13 in Minneapolis in 1955. In the 1955 game, the Gophers had led 13-0.

"I can remember the 1954 game," said Youso. "We were a pretty cocky bunch of freshmen. When the varsity came on the (practice) field for the first time after the loss to Michigan, we were singing the Michigan rouser. They weren't too happy."

A homecoming crowd of 84,639 and the Wolverines were waiting for the Gophers at Michigan Stadium.

GAME OF MY LIFE

BY FRANK YOUSO

Murray kept us in the locker room a long time before the game. We knew Murray wanted to win because of how the game had gone the previous two years, but we didn't know what he was thinking. He had a student manager watching to make sure that Michigan had taken the field first. Finally we took the field and Michigan was on the sideline waiting for us.

We knew it was going to be loud and we prepared for it. But in the first half, the crowd was so noisy we couldn't hear the quarterback.

The crowd was so active in the first half. As we walked onto the field, they were yelling 'Go Blue' and then they would stomp their feet. They kept it up the whole first half.

I had never heard anything so loud as that—'Go Blue. Bang.' The whole ground was shaking our feet. I thought it was a great atmosphere.

We went into the locker room at halftime trailing 7-0. At halftime, Murray told us we were switching to a fast-huddle or no-huddle offense. We had prepared for this in practice, so we were ready.

Our quarterback, Bobby Cox, who was from Walla Walla, Washington, and was my roommate, was outstanding in the second half. We had a pretty good line—(future All-American) Bob Hobert, guards David Burkholder and Bob Rasmussen, Bill Jukich, Dean Maas, Jon Jelacic and Perry Gehring. Everybody did a good job that day.

I think it (the no-huddle offense) really confused Michigan's defense. We didn't let up in the second half. It was just one play right after another. The thing about the no-huddle is you just don't give the defense any time to rest. And every time we ran a play in the second half, it seemed like we were gaining 10 or 12 yards. We didn't give them a chance to catch their breath. It really took their crowd out of the game.

I think it was one of my better games, although I also had a good game against Michigan at home the previous year.

One other thing I remember is the crowd (estimated at 5,000) that greeted us at the airport when we got home. It was quite exciting that many people turned out to greet us.

GAME RESULTS

The Gophers' no-huddle offense even made it difficult for the sportswriters covering the game. Joe Falls wrote in the next day's *Detroit Free Press*, "The scribes were screaming in the press box for Minnesota to slow down so they could keep up with the game."

After seven years of pro football, Frank Youso owned several businesses and helped form the Bronko Nagurski Museum in International Falls, Minnesota.

The only scoring in the first half came when the Wolverines put together a 92-yard drive, but Cox, who had transferred to Minnesota from the University of Washington, scored two touchdowns in the second half to help the Gophers rally for a 20-7 victory.

Trailing 7-0 in the third quarter, the Gophers put together their own 92-yard drive, which was capped by a 30-yard touchdown run by Bob Schultz.

In the fourth quarter, the Gophers took advantage of a Michigan fumble at the Michigan 28 to take the lead. Cox capped that drive with a three-yard touchdown run. Later in the fourth quarter, the Gophers went 55 yards in 10 plays—with the final play being a seven-yard touchdown run by Cox.

Michigan put together a late threat, but an interception by the Gophers' Mike Svendsen at the Gophers' 2-yard line sealed the victory.

Longtime *Minneapolis Tribune* columnist Dick Cullum described the outcome as "one of the most glorious victories in the history of Minnesota football."

Cox finished with 83 yards in 19 carries as the Gophers outrushed Michigan, 243-213, on the ground. But the Wolverines, with future first-round draft choice Ron Kramer as a target, passed for 131 yards to outgain the Gophers, 344-299.

Cox attempted just four passes—completing two for 56 yards—while Michigan completed 10 of 17 passes.

Michigan coach Benny Oosterbaan told the Associated Press, "That quick huddle business threw us off balance. We couldn't straighten our switching defenses, and this made us vulnerable to their runs up center.

Cox credited the play of the Gophers' line to the Associated Press: "That tackling was the best I've ever seen or heard of in a college game. Gehring, Youso, and Hobert were knocking them down so fast blocking and tackling that all we had to do was run over them."

The victory moved the Gophers up to No. 8 in the Associated Press poll, while the Wolverines fell to No. 17. The following week on homecoming, the Gophers outlasted No. 11 Pittsburgh, 9-6, to improve to 5-0-1.

Next on the schedule was Iowa. While the Gophers were outlasting Pittsburgh, Iowa was suffering its first loss of the season, 17-14, to Michigan at home. The No. 15 Hawkeyes, who were 3-5-1 in 1955, were 5-1 overall and 3-1 in the Big Ten.

The winner of the game would have the inside track to the Rose Bowl—a game neither program had played in. The game turned out to be a nightmare for the Gophers, as they committed six turnovers as Iowa held on for a 7-0 victory.

The Gophers concluded the regular season with a 14-13 victory over Michigan State and a 13-13 tie with Wisconsin. Iowa defeated Ohio State the week after beating the Gophers for a 5-1 Big Ten record and a sport in the Rose Bowl.

Had the Gophers (6-1-2, 4-1-2) defeated the Hawkeyes, they would have earned the Rose Bowl berth. Of the Gophers' nine games in 1956, only two had been decided by more than a touchdown. Twice the Gophers won on a field goal in the final minutes and they won another game by one point.

WHAT HAPPENED TO FRANK YOUSO?

The Gophers went into the 1957 season ranked No. 4 in the Associated Press preseason poll. The Gophers started the season with three victories, but stumbled and lost five of their last six games to finish with a disappointing 4-5 record.

Following the 1957 season, Youso was selected by the New York Giants in the second round of the NFL draft. Winnipeg of the CFL, coached by former Gopher Bud Grant, also was interested in signing Youso.

"It came down to the Giants offered me a no-cut contract," said Youso, "so I signed with them."

In his rookie season, the Giants reached the NFL championship game where they played the Baltimore Colts and quarterback Johnny

Unitas. The Colts won the game—considered by many as the greatest game in NFL history—23-17 in overtime—the first overtime game in league history.

"I was the only guy on the field who played both ways," said Youso. "I played just offense in the first half. In the second half, Rosey Grier got hurt for us and our coach Jim Lee Howell was looking up and down the sideline for someone to go in on defense. Vince Lombardi, our offensive coordinator, said, 'Take Youso.' I said I didn't know what to do on defense but I went in and played. I remember asking Sam Huff, our linebacker, 'What should I do?'"

Youso spent two more seasons with the Giants before joining the expansion Minnesota Vikings in 1961.

"I wanted to be closer to home," said Youso. "But playing for (Vikings coach) Norm Van Brocklin was like jumping into a frying pan."

Youso spent two seasons with the Vikings and then spent two seasons with the Oakland Raiders in the AFL before retiring to International Falls.

"We had bought a motel while I was with the Giants," said Youso. "When I got done playing, we bought a resort on Lake Kabetogama. We had that seven years and then sold it. And then I eventually sold the motel too."

In retirement, Youso was instrumental in the formation of the Bronko Nagurski Museum, which is part of the Koochiching County Museum.

Youso spends his time hunting and fishing and watching his grandsons play hockey for the Broncos.

Chapter 6

TOM BROWN

EARLY LIFE OF TOM BROWN

Tom Brown's mother wasn't sure what his favorite sport was, but by the time he was a senior in high school she was certain about one thing.

"When he finishes Central (High School), he's going to Minnesota," Mayme Brown told the *Minneapolis Star* in September of 1953.

Tom Brown was expected to follow in the footsteps of his two older brothers and his mother, who all attended the University.

As an athlete, Brown shared something in common with his brothers. Brown, who competed in football in the fall and track and field in the spring, competed in swimming during the winter. His brothers had competed in swimming for Central but hadn't played football.

"I don't know which sport Tom likes best," Mayme Brown told the *Minneapolis Star*. "In the fall, I think it's football. Then when winter comes and the swimming season starts, I think he likes swimming best. Then comes spring and track. Before the season's over, he makes me think he likes track the best."

Everyone did agree that Brown was an outstanding athlete. Brown credited his winter sport.

"The swimming helped me a lot as an athlete," said Brown.

NAME: Thomas E. Brown
BORN: December 5, 1936
POSITION: Guard
HEIGHT: 6-0
WEIGHT: 240
YEARS: 958-1960
ACCOMPLISHMENTS: First team
   All-Big Ten (1960); Chicago
   Tribune Big Ten MVP (1960);
   first team All-America (1960);
   Outland Trophy winner
   (1960); CFL Hall of Fame
   (1989); College Football Hall
   of Fame (2003).
GAME: vs. Iowa—November 5,
   1960

As a sophomore, Brown helped Central's football team to a 6-1 record, finished fourth at the state swimming meet in the 50-yard freestyle and finished second in the shot put as Central won the state track title.

As a junior, he again led Central to a 6-1 record in football and set a state record in the shot put and was second in the discus as Central repeated as the state champion in track.

His effort of 54-10½ in the shot put broke the record of 54-0½ set by future three-time Olympian Fortune Gordien in 1941. That spring, Brown also had an effort of 55-6½, but only records set at the state meet were considered official state records.

As a senior, he played tackle, linebacker and fullback and earned all-conference honors in football, and finished fourth at the state swim meet in the 100 breaststroke. At the state track meet, he won the discus and finished second in the shot as Central finished third.

Central football coach Joe Markley told the *Minneapolis Star* in September of 1953, "If a coach had 11 men like Brown, he'd never have a thing to worry about. Tom could play any position on the team; he's just that kind of football player."

After graduating, Brown did enroll at the University, but his Gophers career was delayed.

Coach Murray Warmath said that Tom Brown's performance in the 1960 Iowa game was the greatest he'd ever seen.

As a freshman, Brown became friends with a teammate—Dave Burkholder. Brown and Burkholder decided to join the U.S. Navy. Brown visited the Navy recruiting office and enlisted. Later that day, Brown phoned Burkholder and learned that his friend hadn't been serious about enlisting, but Brown went ahead and enlisted. While in the Navy, he played two years of football at Great Lakes Naval Station—just outside of Chicago.

Brown returned to the University campus in the fall of 1957.

SETTING

The Gophers went 4-5 in 1957, but the 1958 and 1959 seasons were very disappointing for the Gophers and coach Murray Warmath. The Gophers went 3-15 in those two seasons, including a 2-12 record in the Big Ten. Ten of the 15 losses were by eight points or less as alumni and students started clamoring for Warmath to be fired.

So, expectations were low for the Gophers heading into the 1960 season. Even after the Gophers opened the 1960 season with a 26-14 victory at home over No. 12 Nebraska, there wasn't much enthusiasm about the Gophers.

But there soon would be.

The victory over Nebraska earned the Gophers a spot in the Associated Press Top 20 poll (No. 18) for the first time in nearly three years—since a No. 14 ranking in mid-October of 1957.

A 42-0 victory over Indiana the following week improved the Gophers to 2-0 and moved them up four spots in the Associated Press poll. Another shutout victory—7-0 over Northwestern— moved the Gophers into the Top 10.

The Gophers remained unbeaten with a 21-10 victory over Illinois. Following the victory, the Gophers moved up to No. 6 in the poll.

Despite their third shutout victory in five weeks—10-0 over Michigan, which ended a three-game losing streak to the Wolverines—the Gophers remained No. 6 in the poll as the five teams ranked above them also won that week.

The Gophers improved to 6-0—for the first time since their national championship season of 1941—with a convincing 48-7 nonconference victory over Kansas State. The victory moved the Gophers to No. 3 in the Associated Press. In the United Press poll, the Gophers were No. 2.

Next up for the Gophers was top-ranked Iowa. The Hawkeyes, who had been ranked No. 15 in the Associated Press preseason poll, were 29-7-2 in the previous four seasons and had won Big Ten titles in 1956 and 1958 (defeating California, 38-12, in the Rose Bowl following the 1958 season).

The Hawkeyes opened the season with a 22-12 victory over No. 10 Oregon State to move up No. 8 in the poll. In their second game, the Hawkeyes routed No. 6 Northwestern, 42-0. That loss dropped Northwestern, which had been ranked No. 14 in the preseason and moved up to No. 6 with an impressive 19-3 victory over Oklahoma, out of the poll.

While the Gophers were defeating Northwestern, 7-0, Iowa, which had moved up to No. 3, defeated Michigan State, 27-15.

The Hawkeyes, now No. 2, followed that victory with a 28-21 victory over No. 12 Wisconsin to improve to 4-0. Even though top-ranked Mississippi had defeated Tulane, 26-13, that week, the Hawkeyes moved into the No. 1 spot.

The Hawkeyes followed up with victories over two ranked opponents—No. 10 Purdue (21-14) and No. 19 Kansas (21-7)—to match the Gophers' 6-0 record.

The Hawkeyes came to Minneapolis with a five-game winning streak over the Gophers. The Hawkeyes had shut out the Gophers three times in the previous five years, while outscoring the Gophers, 138-26.

GAME OF MY LIFE

BY TOM BROWN

Obviously, this was a big game for both of us. Iowa was No. 1 and we were chasing them.

I remember how hyped everybody on campus was. The day before the game, there was a pep rally in front of Northrop Auditorium. I told the fans that we'd give Iowa hell.

I had a pinched nerve in my left shoulder and it was heavily bandaged. But it didn't affect me during the game.

I had always prided myself on getting off the ball quick. Especially when the right guard was pulling because it would leave a hole for me.

I was able to come up with a couple of plays that day that helped us. It was just one of those games. You know it was like Andy Warhol said everybody would have their 15 minutes of fame. That was mine. I played a good game and it kind of led to some awards for me.

But the thing I remember the most is how excited we were that day.

GAME RESULTS

A record Memorial Stadium crowd of 65,610 saw the Gophers pull away in the second half for a 27-10 victory over the Hawkeyes.

One Gophers assistant coach told the *Chicago Tribune*, "you heard Murray (Warmath) say Brown played the greatest game he'd ever seen. I'll tell you that Brown is the greatest lineman I ever coached. I had Bob Ward at Maryland, but Brown has more weight and more strength and moves like a cat."

Brown made an impact against the Hawkeyes almost immediately.

On their first possession, the Hawkeyes advanced from their own 20-yard line to the 49. On 4th-and-15, the Hawkeyes lined up to punt. Center Bill Van Buren, obviously concerned with Brown lined up opposite of him, snapped the ball over punter John Calhoun's head. Calhoun raced to recover the ball, but was tackled at the Iowa 14-yard line. Three plays later, the Gophers scored to take a 7-0 lead.

Tom Brown picked up numerous awards after leading the Gophers to the 1960 national championship.

Brown made his presence felt again in the second quarter. Trailing 7-0, the Hawkeyes started at their own 25-yard line and in 11 plays drove to the Gophers' 6. On third down, Hawkeyes guard Bill DiCindio was driven back into Hawkeyes quarterback Wilbur Hollis by Brown. Hollis was dropped on the 11-yard line and Iowa had to settle for a field goal by Tom Moore.

The Hawkeyes, who trailed 7-3 at halftime, scored on their opening possession of the second half to take a 10-7 lead. But the Gophers went ahead 13-10 after a drive that saw reserve quarterback Joe Salem complete a crucial 28-yard pass.

Iowa fumbled again and the Gophers recovered and responded with Roger Hagberg's 42-yard run for a touchdown. The longest run of the season by a Gopher made it 19-10.

On the ensuing possession, the Hawkeyes fumbled again and Bobby Bell recovered. The Gophers dashed in—on a touchdown run by Salem—for a 27-10 lead.

The victory moved the unbeaten Gophers into the No. 1 spot in the poll, but the Gophers were upset the following Saturday by Purdue and future Minnesota Twins infielder Bernie Allen, 23-14. The loss dropped the Gophers to No. 4 as Missouri took over the top spot. But Missouri, coached by Minnesota native Dan Devine, lost its regular-season finale to Kansas, 23-7.

The Gophers regrouped to win their regular-season finale over Wisconsin, 13-7 while the Hawkeyes closed out the regular season with victories over Ohio State (35-12) and Notre Dame (28-0) to tie the Gophers for the Big Ten title.

In the final regular-season poll, the Gophers returned to the No. 1 spot to claim their first national title since 1941. The Hawkeyes were No. 3.

The Gophers were rewarded with their first-ever trip to the Rose Bowl where they lost to Washington, 17-7.

Brown was the team MVP, runner-up in the Heisman Trophy voting (Navy's Joe Bellino won) and the Outland Trophy winner.

Coach Warmath told the *Minneapolis Tribune* that Brown's play was "the outstanding single factor" in the amazing comeback season of the Gophers. Warmath called Brown the best lineman in the country.

WHAT HAPPENED TO TOM BROWN?

Following his collegiate career, Brown was drafted by the Baltimore Colts of the NFL and the New York Titans of the fledgling AFL.

Brown decided to sign with the British Columbia Lions of the CFL because he preferred "the West Coast with its wilderness and snow-capped mountains. The money was about the same at the time. Of course, about three years later, the NFL contracts shot up. But I was enjoying life, and that was more important than money. At least that's how I rationalized it."

Brown had a successful, but brief career in the CFL. As a linebacker he helped the Lions to the Grey Cup (the CFL championship game) in 1964. But a neck injury led to a premature end to his playing career in 1967.

After the injury, Brown underwent surgery at the Mayo Clinic in Rochester where two cervical discs were fused together.

After his playing career, Brown embarked on a successful career in sales in the Pacific Northwest. He turned his love of the outdoors into a business venture by owning and operating a rafting company.

"I've had a lot of fun," Brown told the *Minneapolis Star Tribune* in December of 2003. "Hey, what else is there?"

In December of 2003, Brown was inducted into the College Football Hall of Fame. Brown was the 19th former Gopher player or coach to earn the honor.

"When the Hall of Fame committee sent me the official letter, there was a note saying that it was 'long overdue.' But it's nice to be remembered now," Brown told the *Minneapolis Star Tribune*.

Warmath told the *Minneapolis Star Tribune*, "Tom Brown was one of the very best football players I have ever seen play, anywhere.

He was a big, strong guy, and fast. The woods ain't full of those kind of guys."

Chapter 7

BOBBY BELL

EARLY LIFE OF BOBBY BELL

Growing up in rural North Carolina in the 1950s limited Bobby Bell's options for playing college football, but Bell is proof that if you've got talent, it will get noticed.

"I grew up in a small town, Shelby—between Charlotte and Asheville," said Bell. "My high school (Cleveland) was small. We only had 26 kids in my graduating class. We played six-man football."

Bell, who was a quarterback in high school, got noticed when he played in an all-star game in Greensboro, North Carolina, catching the attention of North Carolina coach Jim Tatum.

"I was looking at playing at North Carolina A&T," said Bell. "At the all-star game, Tatum saw me talking to a Notre Dame coach. Notre Dame was on North Carolina's schedule the next two seasons. Tatum didn't want me playing at a school that was on his schedule. So he told (Gophers assistant coach) Jim Camp, 'I've got a six-man quarterback. He's a helluva quarterback, but he can play any position for you. I guarantee he'll lead you to a Big Ten championship and the Rose Bowl.'"

Well, the Gopher coaching staff, coming off a 1-8 season, was interested in anyone who could help them. Gophers coach Murray Warmath told the *Minneapolis Star Tribune* years later that it became

NAME: Robert Lee Bell, Jr.
BORN: June 17, 1940
POSITION: Tackle
HEIGHT: 6-4
WEIGHT: 228
YEARS: 1960-1962
ACCOMPLISHMENTS: First team
   All-Big Ten (1961, 1962);
   first team All-America (1961,
   1962); Outland Trophy winner
   (1962); College Football Hall
   of Fame; Pro Football Hall of
   Fame
GAME: vs. Michigan State—
   November 4, 1961

clear to him in the late 1950s that he needed to extend Minnesota's recruiting boundaries, and he decided on Western Pennsylvania and North Carolina, where he had recruited years earlier as an Army assistant.

"They (the Gophers coaching staff) called the principal at my high school and said, 'We'd like to see some film of Bobby before we offer him a scholarship,'" said Bell. "Cleveland was just a small poor school and the principal said, 'We don't have any film, but I can get you some pictures that were in the Shelby newspaper.' That was it. They couldn't believe it."

So Warmath and Camp had Bell work out for the Shelby High School coach.

"He had me run a 40-yard dash, a mile, and throw the ball," said Bell. "He told Minnesota, 'This kid can do it all.' I think I got the Gophers' last available scholarship."

Most of Bell's friends and family wanted him to go to a college near his hometown.

"But my dad said to me, 'It's always been your dream to play football at a big school and get a scholarship. You should do it if you have the chance.' He was my guiding force. He told me to go do it," said Bell.

In high school, Bobby Bell was the quarterback of his six-man football team.

Bell was part of a select group of recruits at Minnesota. Bell joined Sandy Stephens, Bill Munsey, and Judge Dickson as the first group of black recruits at Minnesota.

"It was a situation where it was a pioneer thing," Bell said. "We came to Minnesota and we were all on the same page. We lived in the same dorm and watched out for each other. We couldn't screw up.

"Coming to Minnesota, I had so many people I was accountable to. Not just myself and my family, but all of Shelby. The way I looked at it, there was no way I could go back to Shelby if I quit or it didn't work out."

So in 1959, Bell joined the University of Minnesota freshman football team. Ironically, North Carolina coach Jim Tatum, who was worried about Bell playing for Notre Dame, didn't return as the Tar Heels coach for the 1959 season.

SETTING

When he arrived in Minnesota for his freshman year, Bell was greeted by Stephens and Dickson.

"They met me at the airport. The first thing they said to me was, 'Do you want to go to the Rose Bowl?'" said Bell. "I said yes."

During the 1959 season, the Rose Bowl was just a distant dream for the Gophers, who went 2-7. That first year in Minnesota provided a lot of challenges for Bell on the field, where he had been moved to tackle to take advantage of his quickness, and off the field.

"It was a rough first year," said Bell. "I had just the basics in high school. I really had to burn the midnight oil, studying, to stay eligible.

"But I was really lucky. We had an assistant coach, Butch Nash. He was like a father to me. He would come up to me at practice and say he had checked my grades. He'd say, 'I'm watching you.' He told me, 'If you have a problem with one of your classes we can get you help.' He watched out for me like he would a son."

On the field, things turned around for the Gophers in 1960. Led by Outland Trophy winner Tom Brown, the Gophers went 8-1 and tied for the Big Ten title (with Iowa). A victory over the Hawkeyes, who were ranked No. 1 at the time, helped the Gophers earn their first Big Ten title and national championship since 1941.

The Gophers' reward was a trip to the Rose Bowl—the first bowl game in school history.

The Gophers opened the 1961 season with a 6-0 loss to Missouri. Missouri, which had gone 10-1 in 1960 and won the Orange Bowl, had opened its season a week earlier with a 28-6 victory over Washington State.

The Gophers rebounded to win their next four games—Oregon (14-7), Northwestern (10-3), Illinois (33-0) and Michigan (23-20). The victory over Illinois moved the Gophers to No. 6 in the Associated Press poll and in the victory over Michigan, the Gophers scored two touchdowns in the fourth quarter—the last with 1:24 remaining—to rally. That victory left the Gophers tied for first (with Ohio State and Michigan State) in the Big Ten standings.

Minneapolis Star and *Tribune* executive sports editor Charles Johnson, who had started his sportswriting career in 1916, wrote in the *Minneapolis Sunday Tribune* that the victory "has to rate with the great Gopher triumphs of all time."

The Gophers, who moved up to No. 5 in the poll, turned their attention to Michigan State. The Spartans (5-0 overall, 3-0 in the Big Ten) were ranked No. 1 in the nation. The Spartans, who were No. 6 in the preseason poll, had been in the top spot for three weeks. The Spartans had opened the season with victories over Wisconsin (20-0) and Stanford (31-3) to move up to No. 5. The Spartans were so impressive in a 28-0 victory over Michigan that they moved up to No. 1—even though the four teams ranked above them had won as well.

The Spartans then defeated Notre Dame and Indiana to remain unbeaten. The Spartans, with future All-America running back George Saimes, had a punishing rushing offense and a tough defense. For the season, the Spartans averaged 237.2 yards rushing per game and allowed just 50 points in nine games.

GAME OF MY LIFE

BY BOBBY BELL

For me, personally, all the games are memorable. Just to pick one is awful tough.

I was the type of player who played each game to the best of his ability and then moved on. Some guys can remember every play from every game.

To me, to make my game better, I would study film after the game and then two days later move on to the next game. That's the way I approached it. There are memorable games, losing to Wisconsin in 1962, the two Rose Bowls.

But the game against Michigan State is certainly memorable.

They came into the game averaging, it seemed like, 500 yards per game on the ground. They had one of the best offenses and defenses in the country and the game was going to be televised nationally.

I didn't have a very good game (against Michigan) the week before. I just couldn't get started in that game. Why, I don't know. That week in practice, we were wondering how in the world we were going to play them—stop their running game and block their defensive line. But we really shut them down. We played tough defense all day.

We had scored on our first possession. Sandy (Stephens) drove us 70 yards in 11 plays. We had to drive to about the 25-yard line. We came up to the line, Carl (Eller) and I were supposed to block Ed Budde, who was 6-foot-4 and weighed 245. We were going to run off tackle. He dug in and we maybe moved him two yards. We decided to run the same play again. We came up to the line of scrimmage and I said to Ed, 'I guess you better buckle up.' We wanted to make a point, so we ran the play again. The dirt was really

---

After being switched to tackle to take advantage of his quickness, Bobby Bell developed into a two-time All-American.

piling up. But we thought, 'We can do it.' It was fun blocking against a top-ranked team.

Ed and I became teammates in pro football and I talked to him all the time about that game. Especially the first half. I think we only gave up 26 yards rushing in the first half.

On offense, we surprised them with our unbalanced line. It was the first time in three years Coach Warmath had used the offense. It moved both me and Carl (Eller) to the same side of the ball. I really enjoyed blocking next to Carl.

GAME RESULTS

The Gophers forced three Spartan turnovers and limited the Spartans to 161 yards rushing (in 47 carries for 3.4 yards per carry) in the 13-0 victory. The two touchdowns scored by the Gophers, who didn't commit a turnover, were the first allowed by the Spartans in conference play.

After the Gophers had taken a 7-0 lead, Michigan State got the ball back and drove to the Gophers' 6-yard line. On fourth down, Dave Mulholland and Bell stopped Saimes short of the goal line. In the second quarter, the Spartans drove to the Gophers' 12, and on 4th-and-1, Saimes slipped and fell short of a first down.

The Gophers outgained the Spartans, 293-260, as they rushed for 201 yards. Munsey, who had missed the Gophers' previous two games, rushed for 60 yards and scored both touchdowns. He scored on an 8-yard run and a 23-yard touchdown pass from Stephens. Stephens rushed for 45 yards and completed five passes for 92 yards. On defense, Stephens intercepted a pass.

Spartans coach Duffy Daugherty told the *Minneapolis Sunday Tribune*, "They're a good team ... a very fine team. They pound you on defense and I think they are extremely well-coached. In a close game like this, and we knew it would be close, you can't miss the opportunities that we missed. This kind of football is a game of inches. We were inches short too often."

The Gophers followed with victories over Iowa (16-9) and Purdue (10-7) to improve to 6-0 in the Big Ten and move up to No.

3 in the poll heading into their regular-season finale at home against Wisconsin.

A 23-21 loss to Wisconsin cost the Gophers a share of a second consecutive Big Ten title. Ohio State earned the conference title with a 50-20 victory over Michigan. The Gophers' season appeared over, but the Ohio State University Faculty Council voted to turn down an invitation to the Rose Bowl. As the conference runner-up, the Gophers were invited to play in the game and the school accepted.

The Gophers' second consecutive trip to the Rose Bowl had a more enjoyable outcome than the first. The Gophers, who had lost to Washington 17-7 in the previous Rose Bowl, defeated UCLA, 21-3, for their first-ever bowl victory.

Bell was named first team All-Big Ten and first team All-America after anchoring a defense that finished sixth in the nation in rushing defense (84.3 yards per game).

The Gophers were tough again in 1962. After going 1-1-1 in their first three games, the Gophers won five consecutive games—while allowing just 13 points—to take a 6-1-1 overall record and a 5-1 Big Ten record into their regular-season finale against Wisconsin.

The winner of the game would be the Big Ten champion. A controversial roughing-the-passer call against Bell late in the game helped the Badgers overcome the Gophers, 14-9.

Following the season, Bell was named the Outland Trophy winner and was third in the Heisman Trophy Award voting (behind Oregon State quarterback Terry Baker and LSU halfback Jerry Stovall).

WHAT HAPPENED TO BOBBY BELL?

Uncertain about his professional football future—sign with the Kansas City Chiefs of the upstart AFL or with the Minnesota Vikings of the more established NFL—Bell asked Warmath for his opinion.

Bell told the *Minneapolis Star Tribune* that "he emerged (from the meeting) with a vision of his future."

Bell surprised almost everyone in professional football when he signed with the Chiefs. The Chiefs and the rest of the AFL were so convinced that Bell was going to sign with the Vikings, who had drafted him in the second round, that the Chiefs didn't bother selecting Bell until the seventh round of the draft.

Over the next 12 seasons, Bell was one of the best players in professional football. He spent his first two seasons in pro football as a defensive end before switching to linebacker in 1965. Between 1963-1974, he was named All-AFL/AFC nine times and led the Chiefs to two Super Bowls. In January of 1970, the Chiefs surprised the favored Vikings, 23-7, in Super Bowl IX.

During his career with the Chiefs he intercepted 26 passes and returned six of them for touchdowns. In 1969, he was elected to the All-Time (1960-1969) AFL team. Bell was elected to the Pro Football Hall of Fame in 1983 and the College Football Hall of Fame in 1991. Bell was the first Kansas City Chiefs player to be elected to the Pro Football Hall of Fame.

Following his pro career, Bell owned three restaurants before retiring from business. He continues to make speaking engagements—speaking to businesses about teamwork.

Chapter 8

Coach

MURRAY WARMATH

EARLY LIFE OF MURRAY WARMATH

Warmath was born in a small farming town about an hour northeast of Memphis—the only child of Carl and Imogene Warmath.

Warmath's youth was pretty typical—until he was 10 years old. His mother died that year, and several months later, his father decided to leave Humboldt for a business opportunity.

Warmath stayed in Humboldt and went to live with an aunt and uncle.

Three years later, his aunt passed away and Warmath was sent to live with another aunt and uncle.

During the summers, Warmath worked for another uncle, who was a produce broker.

Warmath attended Humboldt High School through the 11th grade. He played both football and baseball and by the time he was a junior, he was getting noticed on the football field.

For his senior year of high school, Warmath was accepted at Branham-Hughes Military Academy in Spring Hill, Tennessee— thirty miles south of Nashville.

Warmath made the move to help him prepare for college. At Branham, Warmath caught the attention of several Southern schools, including Vanderbilt and Tennessee.

NAME: Murray Warmath
BORN: December 26, 1912
POSITION: Coach
YEARS: 1954-1971
ACCOMPLISHMENTS: Coached
   Gophers to two Rose Bowl
   appearances and a national
   title (1960).
GAME: vs. UCLA in the Rose
   Bowl—January 1, 1962

Warmath eventually decided on the University of Tennessee, where he would play football for the legendary Bob Neyland. Warmath lettered for the Volunteers from 1932-34, and then joined Neyland's staff as an assistant in 1935. He stayed until 1939, when he joined the Mississippi State staff. He was in Starkville, Mississippi, for three years before serving in the Navy during World War II as a communications officer.

He rejoined Neyland's staff and was there from 1945-1949.

In 1949, Warmath went to work for another college football legend —Colonel Earl Blaik at Army. Warmath filled the vacancy on Blaik's staff created when Minneapolis native Sid Gillman left to become the head coach at the University of Cincinnati.

In 1952, Warmath got his first head coaching job—at Mississippi State. After two seasons as the Bulldogs coach—he was named the coach at the University of Minnesota in January of 1954.

Warmath's first squad at Minnesota went 7-2. But the Gophers had losing seasons in four of the next five seasons, and many Gophers fans and alumni began clamoring for Warmath to be replaced. After the Gophers' dismal 1-9 season in 1958, the heat was really turned up on Warmath.

In December of 1958, United Press International reported that a letter, signed by 11 Minnesota legislators and addressed to the University's Board of Regents, asked for the removal of Warmath and Gophers athletic director Ike Armstrong. State Representative Stanley J. Fudro of Minneapolis said, "We would like to have a former University of Minnesota athlete appointed as the head coach. Why should they go so far to get a coach when they have qualified men who are former Minnesota men?"

Murray Warmath (left) was an assistant to two college football legends—Tennessee's Bob Neyland and Army's Earl Blaik—before becoming a head coach in 1952.

The University of Minnesota "M" Club was also very vocal in its dislike of Warmath. When alumni demanded that Warmath and athletic director Ike Armstrong be replaced, the University Board of Regents refused to bow to the pressure. The regents held a four-hour closed-door meeting, after which President James Morrill announced that the board would not fire Warmath and Armstrong. Two weeks later, the "M" Club released a seven-page statement accusing Morrill of misleading them.

Things didn't improve much in 1959 as the Gophers went 3-6. Of the 15 losses for the Gophers in 1958 and 1959—nine were by eight points or less. Students showed their displeasure when Warmath was hung in effigy outside a campus dormitory.

Following the 1959 season, speculation about Warmath's future heated up again. A Twin Cities radio station reported he had agreed to resign if his contract—which had two years remaining worth $37,000—was bought out.

The fans' uneasiness may have peaked at the start of the 1960 season, when the Gophers played poorly in a scrimmage a week before the regular season opened.

But the Gophers opened the season with six consecutive victories before stunning top-ranked Iowa, 27-10, to improve to 7-0. But the following week, the Gophers lost to Purdue, 23-14, in Minneapolis. The Gophers closed out the regular season with a 26-7 victory over Wisconsin.

The Gophers and Iowa finished in a tie for the Big Ten title. Because the Hawkeyes had been to the Rose Bowl in 1956 and 1958, the Gophers were invited to compete. Making their first-ever bowl appearance, the Gophers lost to Washington, 17-7.

SETTING

The Gophers went into the 1961 season with several concerns— who would replace graduated offensive lineman Tom Brown, the Outland Trophy winner and one of the top linemen in school history —and several other key players and a concern about depth.

The Gophers opened the season with a disappointing 6-0 loss to Missouri, coached by Minnesota native Dan Devine, in Minneapolis.

The Gophers regrouped after that loss and won their next seven games. The Gophers gave up more than seven points just twice in that seven-game stretch.

The streak had started slowly. In week two, Oregon led the Gophers, 7-0, at halftime before the Gophers rallied for a 14-7 victory.

After victories over Northwestern and Illinois, the Gophers rallied for a 23-20 victory over Michigan. *Minneapolis Tribune* columnist Dick Cullum called that victory the "most thrilling triumph the Gophers had ever fashioned in this long, lustrous Little Brown Jug rivalry."

The Gophers had trailed 7-0, 13-0 and 20-8 (in the fourth quarter) before Judge Dickson scored the winning touchdown with 1:24 left.

Tribune sports editor Charles Johnson called it one of the Gophers' great triumphs of all time.

The victory over Michigan left the Gophers with a 4-1 overall record and a 3-0 record in Big Ten play. The following week the Gophers played host to undefeated and No. 1 ranked Michigan State. The Spartans had outscored their first three conference opponents, 83-0, and in five games had outscored their opponents, 131-10.

Before a crowd of 59,941, the Gophers stunned Michigan State, 13-0. The Gophers scored touchdowns in the first seven minutes and the last five minutes. The Gophers, who had given up just 36 points in their first five games, forced three turnovers to hand the Spartans their first shutout loss in 25 games.

The Gophers continued to roll as they beat Iowa, which was No. 1 earlier in the season, 16-9, and Purdue.

The Gophers went into their regular-season finale against Wisconsin with a chance to either share the Big Ten title with Ohio State or win it outright if they beat Wisconsin and Michigan beat

Ohio State. But Ohio State defeated Michigan and the Gophers lost out on a share of the title when they lost to Wisconsin, 23-21.

After the loss, the Gophers assumed their season was over. But the day after the game, rumors surfaced that Ohio State might not go to the Rose Bowl. On November 28—three days after the season-finale—the Ohio State Faculty Council voted 28-25 to turn down the Rose Bowl invitation.

On December 1, the University of Minnesota Faculty Senate Committee voted, 108-33, to accept the Rose Bowl Invitation.

According to author Mike Wilkinson, many of the Gopher players weren't too excited about a return trip to the Rose Bowl. Some of the players thought they "had gotten stale" the previous year, which had contributed to the loss to Washington.

Several players talked to Warmath and he agreed things would be looser this time.

GAME OF MY LIFE

BY MURRAY WARMATH

Once we got to Los Angeles, we gave more free time after practice. Everybody was more relaxed and better prepared and not so much in awe of the hoopla that surrounded the game.

I was dealing with rumors that I was going to leave Minnesota to take the head coaching job at Army (Dale Hall had just been fired). We just went about our business.

The previous year against Washington, we dug ourselves an early hole. We fell behind 17-0 at halftime. We wanted to avoid that this time.

UCLA took the opening kickoff and using the running of Kermit Alexander and Bobby Smith drove to our 24. We forced UCLA to kick a field goal and that gave us some breathing room.

Murray Warmath withstood demands for his dismissal in the late 1950s to lead the Gophers to their only Rose Bowl appearances in school history.

Our defense got us going. Late in the first quarter, Judge Dickson recovered a fumble at the UCLA 6-yard line and three plays later Sandy Stephens scored.

When they fumbled at the 6 and we stopped their drive, the ball game was ours. We kept the ball most of the remaining time.

In the second quarter, we put together a 75-yard drive and Bill Munsey scored and we went up 14-3.

In the third quarter our offense sputtered a little, but in the fourth quarter, Stephens directed us on an 11-minute drive—all on the ground. Stephens capped the drive with a 2-yard run and we went on to win the game, 21-3.

We had a big advantage in ball possession (66 plays to 42 plays) and except for a fumbled punt; our mistakes were never at a critical point of the game or in our territory. In the end, we just physically whipped them.

We went into the game with a plan to throw more than 11 passes (number of attempts by Stephens) but we found we could move the ball playing a conservative game plan. When you have an 11-point lead, as we did most of the game, the best thing is to play it safe.

We wouldn't have gone very far offensively without Stephens. He was not only a great field general but also a fine kicker, ball carrier and passer.

This is a game where we got the breaks and won. The few errors we made didn't happen in dangerous territory—UCLA's did. That was the difference in this ballgame.

We played as well as any game during the season. We had felt very confident going into the game. This win rated as one of the most satisfying (of my career).

GAME RESULTS

The Gophers followed up the consecutive trips to the Rose Bowl with another solid season in 1963. After three games, the Gophers were just 1-1-1. But they won five consecutive games to improve to 6-1-1 heading into their regular-season finale at Wisconsin.

The Gophers went into the game ranked No. 5, while the Badgers and quarterback Ron Vanderkelen were ranked No. 3. The teams were tied for first place in the Big Ten standings with 5-1 records.

The Badgers—aided by a controversial penalty against the Gophers late in the game—pulled out a 14-9 victory over the Gophers. The loss cost the Gophers a third consecutive trip to the Rose Bowl by the Gophers.

In the next four seasons, the Gophers finished ninth, fourth, third and fifth in the Big Ten. The Gophers tied (with Purdue and Indiana) for the Big Ten title in 1967. A loss to Purdue was the only one in seven conference games. A week after losing to Purdue, the Gophers routed Indiana, which went to the Rose Bowl, 33-7.

Warmath coached the Gophers for four more seasons—stepping down after consecutive losing seasons in 1969, 1970 and 1971. Warmath's final game as head coach was a 23-21, come-from-behind victory over Wisconsin. In 18 seasons, Warmath coached the Gophers to an 86-78-7 record. In Big Ten play, the Gophers were 66-57-4 under Warmath. The Gophers finished in the top three of the conference seven times in 18 seasons. Warmath's 18 seasons are the second-longest tenure in school history and he is third (behind Dr. Henry Williams and Bernie Bierman) in career victories.

From 1971 to 1978, Warmath served as an assistant to University of Minnesota athletic director Paul Giel.

In the spring of 1978, at the age of 65, Warmath returned to the sidelines as a defensive line coach for the Minnesota Vikings. He retired from coaching in 1980 and became a scout for the Vikings. He continued to work as a scout and doing commentary on Gopher radio broadcasts past his 80th birthday.

WHAT HAPPENED TO MURRAY WARMATH?

In the fall of 2006, at the age of 93, Warmath was elected to the Minnesota Sports Hall of Fame and honored at halftime of the Gophers' homecoming game against Indiana.

Warmath always refused to take credit for the football accomplishments of his players.

"The teams that have the best players usually win," said Warmath. "It's like a horse race. You can't ride a donkey and win the Kentucky Derby."

Warmath had been one of the first college football coaches nationally to recruit black athletes. In the late 1950s and early 1960s, the South was still segregrated.

The 1960 Gophers team included five blacks—Stephens, Judge Dickson and Bob McNeil (who had arrived in 1959) and Bobby Bell and Bill Munsey. In the early 1960s, he added recruits like Carl Eller and McKinley Boston (from North Carolina) and Aaron Brown (from Texas).

Stephens, from Uniontown, Pennsylvania, was the first black quarterback to start at a Big Ten school and became the first black All-American at a major college.

While being recruited by the Gophers, Dickson asked Warmath why he should believe this coach with Southern roots wouldn't discriminate against blacks. "He looked me in the eye and said, 'Well Judge, the only people I discriminate against are people that can't play football.'"

Bell, a member of the College and Pro Football Halls of Fame who lettered three years for the Gophers and won the Outland Trophy in 1962, said, "Murray Warmath said, 'We are going to win with these players,' and that's what he did."

Chapter 9

BOB STEIN

EARLY LIFE OF BOB STEIN

Bob Stein's experience in youth sports was pretty typical.

"My dad coached me," said Stein, "like a lot of kids' dads did."

Stein's father, who had earned a bronze star during World War II as a member of the signal corps in Europe under Gen. Patton, owned an upholstery business with his brother-in-law.

The elder Stein, who had grown up in St. Paul, operated his business in downtown Minneapolis and moved his family to St. Louis Park.

"In high school, I played football and I was a wild pitcher in baseball for a couple of years," said Stein. "In my senior year, I went out for track. I ended up winning the discus title at the state meet and we won the state title. It was pretty exciting."

During his senior year, Stein, who was a very good student, was being recruited by several schools.

"Coming out of high school, I was hoping for an academic scholarship," said Stein, "to an Ivy League school like Harvard, Yale, or Princeton or (Big Ten schools) Minnesota or Northwestern.

"What it came down to was it was important to me that my father be able to see me play."

But Stein's father never saw him play a varsity game for the Gophers.

NAME: Robert Allen Stein
BORN: January 22, 1948
POSITION: End
HEIGHT: 6-3
WEGHT: 235
YEARS: 1966-1968
ACCOMPLISHMENTS: First team
All-America (1967, 1968);
First team All-Big Ten (1967,
1968); Academic All-America
(1967, 1968); Academic All-
Big Ten (1967, 1968); played
eight years in the NFL.
GAME: vs. Utah—September 23,
1967

"In February of my freshman year (freshmen weren't eligible then), I got a call that my father had suffered a heart attack," said Stein. "By the time I got to the hospital he was gone.

"I was devastated when my dad died. Everyone was so supportive. All of the coaches went to my dad's funeral and they didn't even know him. The ensuing times were tough. I was angry at the world. During one practice, (assistant coach) Bob Bossons came up to me. He was a hard-nosed guy that could scare the crap out of you. He said to me, 'Not only do we think you're going to make it (on the field), you're going to make it big.' It was really supportive."

Six months later, while dealing with the loss of his father, Stein suffered a setback.

"I got mono right at the end of the summer," said Stein. "I was so anxious to play, but instead of being able to practice, I was in bed. I was still ticked off at the world, and then I had gotten this. I couldn't play until the fourth game."

Bob Stein excelled as a defensive end (All-America in 1967 and 1968) and the classroom (Academic All-America in 1967 and 1968) during his Minnesota career.

SETTING

Stein finally made his Gopher debut against the Indiana Hoosiers in Bloomington, Indiana, on October 8, 1966 but not before "going nuts."

"During the first quarter, I was sitting on the bench," said Stein. "It was really frustrating. I stood up and went over to Bossons and took his arm and yelled at him, 'I didn't come here to sit on the bench.' Now, I had no business saying that. I had only been practicing a week. He looked at me like I was a crazy lunatic and he said, 'We'll get you in there in the second quarter.' I got to play the rest of the game (which ended in a 7-7 tie).

The next week brought the Iowa Hawkeyes to town for the Gophers' homecoming game.

"(Coach) Murray (Warmath) always called Iowa our most hated rival," Stein said. "That week he had moved Charley Sanders from defensive end to tight end. I started and wanted to play the whole game.

"I ended up playing three quarters. I got clipped and ended up suffering a season-ending knee injury. Oh boy, did that let air out of my balloon. There was torn cartilage."

Stein had made the most of his three quarters of action against the Hawkeyes. Stein had 14 tackles—10 unassisted—and had kicked a field goal in the Gophers' 17-0 victory over the Hawkeyes.

Besides Stein's efforts, the game, in front of a crowd of 62,631, was highlighted by junior guard Ed Duren's school-record 95-yard interception return for a touchdown.

The *Chicago Tribune's* account of the game said, "Michigan scouts present in anticipation of Minnesota's Little Brown Jug visit to Ann Arbor Saturday doubtless will give much space to today's deeds by Stein and (John) Wintermute. Stein, 18, 6-foot-3 and 230 pounds, was all over the place defensively."

At the time of his injury, Stein was leading the Big Ten with eight tackles for losses. At the end of the season, despite playing just six quarters, he was still third in the conference in that category.

"That season was really a rollercoaster for me," said Stein.

It was for the Gophers as well. The victory over Iowa gave the Gophers a 2-2-1 record. The following week, Michigan reclaimed the Little Brown Jug with a 49-0 victory over the Gophers. It was the Gophers' worst loss in 16 years—since a 48-0 loss to Ohio State in 1950.

But the Gophers rebounded from the Michigan loss with victories over Ohio State (17-7) and Northwestern (28-13) to improve to 4-3-1. But the Gophers' season ended with back-to-back losses to Rose Bowl-bound Purdue (16-0) and Wisconsin (7-6). The Gophers' 4-5-1 record was the just the Gophers' second losing season since 1959.

Going into the 1967 season, the Gophers were a young team with a lot of question marks. Purdue, which had been to the Rose Bowl (beating USC, 14-13) the previous season, was the favorite. Purdue had a lot of good players back. Bob Griese was gone, but they had Mike Phipps and LeRoy Keyes.

And Indiana, which had won just one Big Ten game in each of the previous two seasons, would end up surprising a lot of people in 1967 with a strong sophomore class, which included quarterback Harry Gonso and running back John Isenbarger.

GAME OF MY LIFE

BY BOB STEIN

Before our first game, Coach Warmath was asked about the veteran players he had coming back. He was asked to rate the returning veterans and he talked about some players, but he didn't mention me.

When the reporter asked why he didn't mention me, Coach Warmath said, "He only played two games for us last year. I don't know how to rate him." He didn't know what to think about me. I had 14 tackles in my first start, but I was so emotional. I still had all those emotions and couldn't contain them.

Utah had a big and strong team. Their quarterback (Jack Gehrke) was 5-1 as a starter the previous season before he got hurt. (Utah went 0-4 without him in the lineup and finished 5-5).

The game was scoreless in the first half. Our offense had the ball nine times but only crossed midfield (to the Utah 48) once. (Utah threatened twice, but Dennis Hale intercepted a pass in the end zone and the Utes' other drive stalled on the Gophers' 22).

On its first possession of the second half, Utah drove to our 37. They decided to go for it on fourth-and-seven and I hit the quarterback just as he was throwing the ball and it went incomplete (Gehrke was injured on the play and did not return).

We scored to make it 7-0, but they went ahead, 12-7. They had the ball and were down at our 6 with three minutes to go and it looked like we were going to lose.

But I hit the quarterback (third-string quarterback Tim Collins), as he was making a pitch-out on an option play and Hale recovered the fumble.

Phil Hagan (who hadn't entered the game until the fourth quarter and was the third quarterback used by Warmath) drove us down the field, hitting one key pass to Sanders before hitting Chip Litten with a 28-yard touchdown pass to give us the lead with 77 seconds to go.

But I missed the extra point (according to newspaper accounts the attempt was wide right). Utah got the ball back and they started at their 33 and drove to our 35, but I sacked (Collins) on fourth down.

We were fortunate to win the game. We had been outplayed. As a team, you couldn't look at the stats and say we hadn't been outplayed.

Coach Warmath was intense and tough and scared everybody. But he wasn't a screamer. He didn't yell at us at halftime. If you made mistakes he was on your butt and in your face often. If you made a mistake, you avoided him. His assistants were tough too. My position coach (Butch Nash) was probably the best assistant coach in the Big Ten.

GAME RESULTS

Despite being outgained, 378-207, and managing only 10 first downs (five in the last three minutes), the Gophers survived with a 13-12 victory over the Utes. Stein had 11 tackles (four solo) and had a game-high three tackles for losses (for a minus-17 yards).

The following week, the Gophers lost at Nebraska, 7-0, before going on a five-game winning streak. The Gophers took a 6-1 overall record (4-0 in the Big Ten) record into their game at Purdue.

The Gophers, Purdue and Indiana were tied for the Big Ten lead. The Boilermakers defeated the Gophers, 41-12, while Indiana edged Michigan State, 14-13, to retain a share of first place.

The following week, the Gophers rebounded to hand unbeaten and No. 5-ranked Indiana a 33-7 defeat. The victory kept the Gophers' Rose Bowl hopes alive.

The Gophers closed out the regular season by playing host to rival Wisconsin while Purdue and Indiana met in Bloomington. If the Gophers beat the winless Badgers (0-8-1) as expected, and Purdue defeated Indiana as expected, the Gophers would go to the Rose Bowl (at the time the Big Ten champion could not make back-to-back trips to the Rose Bowl).

The Gophers defeated Wisconsin, 31-14, but Indiana, a 14-point underdog, beat Purdue, 19-14, to force a three-way tie for the Big Ten title. Because Indiana had never been to the Rose Bowl, the Hoosiers earned the trip to Pasadena.

"During the game, it was announced Indiana had won," said Stein. "After the game in the locker room, it was like we had lost the game or we had gotten our butts kicked."

After the season Stein was named first team All-Big Ten and All-America.

The Gophers opened the 1968 season against USC and O.J. Simpson. The Gophers led 20-16 (after one of the most memorable plays in Gopher history—an 83-yard kickoff return for a touchdown following a lateral) with about seven minutes to go, but Simpson and the Trojans rallied for a 29-20 victory. Simpson, who scored four touchdowns, rushed for 236 yards and had 365 all-purpose yards.

The Gophers lost the next week to Nebraska, 17-14, but won six of their final eight games to finish with a 6-4 record.

Stein again earned All-Big Ten and All-America honors.

"I didn't play the way I thought I could (in his senior year) because of injuries," said Stein. "I had a bad ankle sprain the last three or four games. Two years ago, when I was having knee replacement, my doctor said, 'When did you break your ankle?' I said I hadn't but that I had a bad sprain when I was a senior. He said, 'Let me show you the fracture line.'"

WHAT HAPPENED TO BOB STEIN?

Stein, the seventh Gopher to earn All-America honors more than once, had a choice to make in 1969—England or pro football.

"I had been offered a Rhodes Scholarship (which would have taken him to Oxford)," said Stein, who graduated from the University with a degree in political science. "I hoped to get drafted as high as I could."

Stein was selected in the fourth round of the draft by the Kansas City Chiefs. In his rookie season, the Chiefs advance to Super Bowl IV where they played the Minnesota Vikings. The Chiefs, who were considered the underdog by as many as 14 points, defeated the Vikings, 23-7).

"That was a pretty good team," said Stein. "Five of the guys are in the Hall of Fame and there were some—like Otis Taylor—who deserve to be in there. I think the Chiefs were motivated about losing the first Super Bowl (to Green Bay) and hearing they played in a junior league."

While playing for the Chiefs, Stein began attending law school on a full-time basis. Stein graduated in the top 10 percent of his law class in 1973.

Stein, who spent four years with the Chiefs, played with the Los Angeles Rams (1973-74) before splitting the 1975 season between the San Diego Chargers and Vikings. In 1976, Stein was traded to New Orleans.

Stein, who began practicing law part-time in 1974 and full-time in 1976, devoted much of his practice in the pro sports area.

In 1987, Stein was named president of the expansion Minnesota Timberwolves. Stein's duties included the complete organization of the franchise, which would begin play in 1989, and overseeing development of the team and the building of a new arena.

"I'm happy I did it," Stein said, "but I wouldn't want to do it again. It was one of the most ambitious projects in pro sports history. The Twin Cities was the smallest market to have the (other) three major sports and a major Division I college program.

"We were building our own arena with no subsidy. Then, two months into our first season, Midwest Federal collapsed and it cost (the franchise) $15 million. So my third full-time job became finding a way to replace the financing at a time the lending market was shrinking. And I had four kids.

"But it was fun being part of bringing something significant to my community."

In 1994, the Timberwolves were sold to Glen Taylor.

"I stayed on for a year (after the sale)," Stein said. "The transition was very amicable and cooperative."

After taking some time off and doing some charity work, Stein went into private business—running a cell phone company and an internet animation company.

Stein also served as a consultant in the telecommunications industry.

Chapter 10

DOUG KINGSRITER

EARLY LIFE OF DOUG KINGSRITER

The 1960s was a great time to be a student at Richfield High School according to Doug Kingsriter.

"We had wonderful programs and administrative staff," said Kingsriter. "Our principal (Gene Olive) was the former baseball coach. He was a great handler of kids and he loved students. It was great preparation for going to college. There was a lot going on. You had to pay attention and do your homework. We had more than 900 kids in our graduating class. It was quite a machine."

Richfield, the largest school in the state at the time, was not only an academic machine but it was an athletic machine as well, turning out good teams and athletes.

Kingsriter, whose father, Arvid, was a minister, flourished in that environment.

"I was encouraged to play sports," said Kingsriter. "My favorite was whatever was in season. I loved baseball. I played basketball, but I wasn't great. I remember something my mother said to me when I was in seventh grade.

"She said, 'Did you know you can get a college scholarship for playing football?' We didn't have a lot of money. That became my ticket to college."

NAME: Douglas James Kingsriter
BORN: January 29, 1950
POSITION: Tight end
HEIGHT: 6-2
WEIGHT: 222
YEARS: 1970-1972
ACCOMPLISHMENTS: First team All-Big Ten and first team All-America (1971).
GAME: vs. Wisconsin—November 20, 1971

As a junior, Kingsriter started getting letters from colleges. By the time he was a senior, he was getting lots of letters.

"I remember telling Sid Hartman (of the *Minneapolis Tribune*)," said Kingsriter, "that I was going to focus on football."

Kingsriter considered a number of schools.

"I was interested in Colorado and Pac-10 schools," said Kingsriter. "Harvard was recruiting me, but I didn't make that visit. I finally chose Minnesota. As a kid, I had listened to Halsey Hall (on Gophers football radio broadcasts). I had always dreamed of playing Michigan. Having (Gophers coach) Murray Warmath in our living room was very special. It really was the only choice."

Besides the Gophers football tradition, one other factor played into Kingsriter's decision.

"I had become involved in the Fellowship of Christian Athletes (FCA) in high school," said Kingsriter. "It became part of my decision-making process for school. I wanted to play where it would be a part of my life.

"My high school athletic director introduced me to it. One day he took me out of class and took me to a luncheon where Wisconsin basketball coach John Erickson spoke about it. It (FCA) was the right fit for me. I was very thankful for the camaraderie and friendships that have lasted a lifetime. It was very beneficial for me.

Tight end Doug Kingsriter led the Gophers in receiving three consecutive seasons.

I wouldn't have known about it if my athletic director hadn't taken me out of class that day."

Kingsriter was named to the all-state high school football team in 1967 and was also all-state in baseball. The Spartans finished third in the state in 1967.

Once he got to the University of Minnesota, his athletic career got off to a slow start. After playing quarterback in high school, Kingsriter was switched to a new position when he joined the Gophers freshman team in the fall of 1968.

"Murray moved me to center," Kingsriter told the *Minneapolis Star*. "He said I'd get a chance to handle the ball on every play, be first out of the huddle and always be on the traveling team. That was not enough for me. I got switched to tight end my sophomore year."

THE SETTING

With his new position, Kingsriter's Gophers career was again delayed.

In the Gophers' final scrimmage before the 1969 season opener, Kingsriter suffered a broken wrist. He sat out the Gophers' 4-5-1 season as a medical redshirt.

The 1970 season saw the Gophers unveil a new Tartan Turf playing surface at Memorial Stadium, and Kingsriter finally got the chance to play.

In his debut, he caught a 20-yard pass on his first play and went on to catch six passes that day.

He went on to catch 26 passes for 362 yards and two touchdowns for the season, which saw the Gophers struggle to a 3-6-1 mark. The six losses were the most by the Gophers since the 1963 and meant back-to-back losing seasons for the first time since 1958 and 1959.

The 1970 season ended with a 39-14 loss to the Badgers in Madison, Wisconsin. In that game, the Badgers took a late time out before scoring a final touchdown.

The 1971 season—Warmath's 18th as the Gophers coach—featured an 11-game schedule for the first time. A scheduling quirk saw the Gophers open with a conference game.

The Gophers opened the season on a positive note as they defeated Indiana, 28-0. Gophers quarterback Craig Curry, who led the Big Ten in total offense the previous season, threw three touchdown passes as the Gophers turned each of four Indiana turnovers into touchdowns. Kingsriter's 11-yard touchdown reception—following a Hoosiers fumble at their own 12-yard line—gave the Gophers a 13-0 lead early in the second quarter.

The following week, the Gophers traveled to Lincoln, Nebraska, to face the top-ranked and defending national champion Nebraska Cornhuskers. The Cornhuskers defeated the Gophers, 35-7, en route to another national championship.

The next week, the Gophers lost to Washington State, 31-20, at home to fall to 1-2 before defeating Kansas, 38-20. A 27-13 loss to Purdue dropped the Gophers to 2-3, but they again evened their record with a 19-14 victory over the Iowa Hawkeyes in Iowa City.

A homecoming loss to No. 4 Michigan started a four-game losing streak. After the loss to the Wolverines, the Gophers suffered a heartbreaking, 14-12 loss to No. 10 Ohio State. Curry had scored on a two-yard touchdown run with 39 seconds remaining to pull the Gophers within two. The Gophers went for the tie, but officials ruled Curry was stopped short of the end zone on his attempt.

Back-to-back losses on the road—to Northwestern and Michigan State—left the Gophers with a 3-7 record. The Badgers, coached by John Jardine, were coming off a 35-27 loss to Illinois and took a 4-5-1 record into the game.

Rumors began circulating in the Twin Cities media in the week leading up to the game that Warmath might be dismissed after the game. The Gophers were assured of their third consecutive losing season for the first time since 1957-59.

Three days before the game, the *Minneapolis Tribune's* Sid Hartman wrote about the rumors surrounding Warmath. But Kingsriter said the rumors weren't mentioned in practice or any of the players meetings that week. University of Minnesota President

Malcolm Moos spoke to the team in the locker room before the game and made no mention of Warmath's status.

The Gophers, who had at least 11 players suffer season-ending injuries during the season, went into the Wisconsin game with 10 seniors slated to start on offense. The only non-senior in the offensive starting lineup was Kingsriter.

GAME OF MY LIFE

BY DOUG KINGSRITER

When I think of the game, two pictures come to mind. The first is of the defense running off the field after stopping the Badgers to give us the ball back late in the game and the second is of us getting into the huddle for the last drive.

This was the last game I would be playing with the class of players who came to the university together. I had an extra year due to an injury redshirt and would go on to another season, and as we were to find out, with a different coach. So the game had sentimental value to me, and it was a jubilant celebration in the endzone with Mel Anderson—a moment of victory for all of us that we were ending this trek we had started together on such a great note.

It was really all about us as a group. The defense had stopped (Wisconsin running back Rufus) Ferguson and as they came off the field the offense knew they had given it all they had to get us the ball. It was their last contribution as seniors and the sense of "We started this together, we're ending this together with an outcome we want."

I remember that we looked at each other in the huddle on the twenty and said we were "going to do this." We were down by five (21-16), so a field goal was not an option. We all knew where the ball had to be before the clock ran out and there was an absolute resolve on each of our parts to do what we had to do to get this win, in spite of the injuries, the wind, and the 80 yards.

Doug Kingsriter was named the National Collegiate Athlete of the Year by the Fellowship of Christian Athletes in 1973.

I caught a 17-yard pass from Craig on the first play of the drive and that added more confidence to the resolve. Curry then completed an 11-yard pass to George Honza and then a nine-yard pass to me got us into Wisconsin territory. We were at the Wisconsin 43-yard line, and it was 4th-and-1 and our offensive line blew open the hole for Ernie Cook because only the end zone was going to stop us. Cook's 14-yard run gave us a first down at the Wisconsin 29 with 52 seconds remaining. Mel made a big play (a 17-yard reception on 3rd-and-10) to get us in the red zone, and I remember Craig looking at Mel in the huddle with a nod for the final pass. Mel ran the route of his life and got both feet in. We converged on him in the end zone—it was a joyous affirmation of our resolve to go out with a great win. It was a special game for the guys who had been together for three years.

The celebration continued in the locker room. We were hugging … there were tears. Captain Bill Light was crying he was so happy. In retrospect, the game was a gift to all of us—the tears of joy washed away a lot of frustration that day. Murray Warmath the coach became Murray Warmath the person to us, because he too had joined us in the hugging and tear-shedding. Any question we were a team was answered in that final scene.

GAME RESULTS

Trailing, 21-16, the Gophers took possession of the ball at their own 20-yard line with 2:08 remaining. Six of their previous possessions had ended without a first down, and the Gophers faced a 20-mph wind (with gusts to 41 mph).

But the Gophers, led by Curry, put together a 12-play, 80-yard drive—capped by a 12-yard touchdown pass to Anderson with nine seconds remaining—to rally for a 23-21 victory. It was the first touchdown reception of his career for Anderson, a senior playing his final game as a Gopher.

Curry was 5-for-9 for 66 yards on the winning drive. For the game, Curry completed 12-of-27 passes for 206 yards. Kingsriter, who caught two passes for 26 yards on the drive, finished with three receptions for 37 yards.

Shortly after the finale, Kingsriter, who finished the season with numbers almost identical to the previous season (28 receptions, 379 yards and two touchdowns), was named first team All-Big Ten and first team All-America.

"That was a total surprise," said Kingsriter. "There were so many good tight ends—like Billy Joe Dupree (Michigan State), J.V. Cain (Colorado), and Charlie Young (USC). It was quite an honor."

The All-America honor included a trip to New York City for an appearance on the Bob Hope television show. Kingsriter joined other first team All-Americans like (future Minnesota Vikings running back) Ed Marinaro of Cornell, (Heisman Trophy winner) Pat Sullivan of Auburn, and Oklahoma running back Greg Pruitt.

Several days after Kingsriter's trip to New York City, former Gopher All-American Paul Giel was introduced as the new athletic director (replacing Marsh Ryman). Giel's first announcement was that Warmath would not return as coach. Cal Stoll was hired to replace Warmath, who became an assistant to Giel.

The Gophers opened the 1972 season with five consecutive losses (including losses to Top Ten teams Colorado and Nebraska). The Gophers, who were 1-7 after eight games, finished the season with consecutive victories over Northwestern, Michigan State, and Wisconsin.

In Stoll's veer offense, Kingsriter still led the team in receiving with 16 catches for 178 yards. It was the third consecutive season he had led the Gophers in receiving. At the time of his graduation, Kingsriter was the school's all-time leader for receptions by a tight end (70). Through the 2006 season, Kingsriter was tied (with Jay Carroll) for third (behind Matt Spaeth and Ben Utecht) for career receptions by a tight end.

Kingsriter, who was named the National Collegiate Athlete of the Year by the FCA in 1973, was selected by the Minnesota Vikings in the sixth round (the 139th player selected overall) of the 1973 draft. Kingsriter made the talent-loaded Vikings roster as a rookie and spent the next three seasons with the Vikings.

"It was such a positive experience," said Kingsriter. "Those were the Super Bowl years and there were such great people on the team. Even though I was there for just a short period—I suffered a knee injury in my third season that ended my career—I learned so much. I was so fortunate to have played for Murray Warmath and Bud Grant, and my high school coach—Bob Collison—was great too."

WHAT HAPPENED TO DOUG KINGSRITER?

Following his playing career, Kingsriter went into the real estate business. Kingsriter built the business into an operation with 10 branch offices before selling the company.

"Our son was born with a congenital heart defect," said Kingsriter. "After his last surgery, when he was four, when we knew he would be okay, we decided on some changes in our life."

Kingsriter and his wife, Debbie, who he met at a FCA speaking engagement in Oklahoma while he was in college, went into the publishing business and wrote children's books and musicals.

"We decided to give back to the community," said Kingsriter. "The musicals were based on scripture and from our hearts and experiences."

In the early 1990s, the Kingsriters and their three children moved to Dallas.

"Deb had lost her mother and her father was ill," said Kingsriter, who went to work as a marketing person for MADD.

"I hadn't been an employee in a long time, so I only signed a one-year contract," said Kingsriter. "I ended up staying seven years. That was my first foray into a non-profit. Then I went to work for a childhood cancer organization. We had offices in Los Angeles and Washington and I ended up commuting a lot."

In 2005, Kingsriter went to work for the Lance Armstrong Foundation.

"We're trying to change the experience of people living with cancer," said Kingsriter. "We're not a research organization. We help people live with cancer. We kick in the moment there is a diagnosis. I really enjoy the work."

Kingsriter is currently a vice president for the Minneapolis Heart Institute Foundation.

Chapter 11

TONY DUNGY

EARLY LIFE OF TONY DUNGY

Dungy was exposed to Big Ten football at an early age—his hometown of Jackson, Michigan, is not far from both the Michigan State University and University of Michigan campuses.

While in grade school, Dungy got a closer look at the Michigan State campus.

"My dad was working on his Ph.D. at Michigan State," said Dungy, "and for three years, my third to fifth grade years, we lived on the Michigan State campus.

"I was there the year (1966) of the 10-10 tie against Notre Dame and the national championship. (Michigan State coach) Duffy Daugherty was an icon (Daugherty coached the Spartans to a 109-69-5 record from 1954-1972)."

The Dungy family returned to Jackson where Dungy said, "There were two ways you could go. You could try to make it in athletics or you could try to be king of the street. I was lucky. My parents (Wilbur, a college instructor, and Cleo, a high school English teacher) established for me that I didn't have to hustle on the street to make it.

"My father had been a boxer. A state Golden Gloves champion. He helped me get into athletics. Everybody has role models. I had heroes in athletics. But I could also look at my dad and see that he

<table>
<tr><td>

NAME: Tony Dungy
BORN: October 6, 1955
POSITION: Quarterback
HEIGHT: 6-1
WEIGHT: 188
YEARS: 1973-1976
ACCOMPLISHMENTS: Two-time
team MVP; second team All-
Big Ten, 1975-76.
GAME: vs. Wisconsin—November
22, 1975

</td></tr>
</table>

went to school and things were paying off for him. I could see some sense in going to school. I was lucky."

Dungy's first passion in high school was basketball, and he said he didn't get "turned on to football until 11th grade" but he became an outstanding three-sport athlete at Jackson's Parkside High School.

His senior year, he was elected class president and was an All-American in football and All-State in basketball. The nine-time letterwinner also competed in baseball and track.

"When I was a senior, I was all set to go to Michigan State," said Dungy, who was recruited by more than 70 schools. "It was not an issue about where I was going. But about midseason (in the fall of 1972), Daugherty announced he was retiring. Michigan State had a long process of selecting a new coach that caught us by surprise.

"While Michigan State was in this long transition period, Cal Stoll was in his first year as the Minnesota coach. He had been an assistant to Daugherty (for 10 years). He came in and recruited seven good players from Michigan that year. My high school coach (Dave Driscoll) knew him. I took a (recruiting) trip to Minnesota and looked around the Twin Cities and fell in love with the area."

Dungy also considered the University of Michigan.

"When I was at Michigan, Bo Schembechler said it would be a miracle if I played before Dennis Franklin," said Dungy. "I appreciated his honesty."

Coach Cal Stoll, who had been an assistant at Michigan State for 10 years, convinced Michigan native Tony Dungy to play for the Gophers.

In early April of 1973, Dungy signed a national letter of intent to play for the Gophers.

"I liked the challenge at Minnesota," said Dungy. "I wanted to get in a program where I could help bring it up."

SETTING

Dungy's transition to college quarterback wasn't without some difficult moments.

As a freshman in 1973, Dungy started one game—on his 18th birthday—against No. 2 Nebraska in Lincoln, Nebraska Dungy rushed for 84 yards in Stoll's Veer-T offense, but was just 5 of 18 for 33 yards with two interceptions in a 48-7 loss to the Cornhuskers. Dungy scored the Gophers' lone touchdown (which made it 7-7 late in the first quarter).

For the season, Dungy was 8 of 33 (24 percent) for 97 yards. He rushed for 251 yards and three touchdowns.

"About the middle of my freshman year, I started to have my doubts," said Dungy. "I didn't know if I'd ever be good enough. People were starting to say I couldn't play or that the Gophers couldn't win until they got a different quarterback. But Coach Stoll kept faith in me."

Dungy rewarded that faith.

The Gophers expected to be entertaining and potent on offense in 1974 with Dungy, Rick Upchurch. and Larry Powell, who had averaged 5.1 yards per carry as a freshman in 1973. But in March of 1974, Powell came down with a rare illness, which was eventually diagnosed as French Polio. Powell went from 180 pounds to 124 pounds and never played football again.

At the beginning of the 1974 season, Stoll said, "Dungy is going to be a great quarterback. He's very bright and one of the most dedicated athletes I've coached. He watches game films so much you have to turn off the lights and kick him out of the building. The thing that scares me is he's smarter than I am."

The Gophers opened the season by playing host to No. 4 Ohio State. The Buckeyes built a 21-3 lead at halftime. Dungy helped the

Gophers pull within nine, 28-19, with five and a half minutes remaining before the Buckeyes prevailed, 34-19.

The following week, Dungy threw four touchdown passes to tie a school record (set by Sandy Stephens in 1961) in the Gophers' 42-30 victory over North Dakota.

The Gophers were 3-3 before losing four of their final five games to finish with a 4-7 record.

Dungy had shown improvement as a sophomore—passing for 612 yards (completing 41 percent of his passes) and rushing for 417 yards. The improvement continued in his junior season.

The Gophers opened the 1975 season with a 20-14 loss to Indiana, but regrouped to win three consecutive nonconference games. Losses to Illinois and Michigan State left the Gophers with a 3-3 record—0-3 in the Big Ten.

Following the loss to Michigan State, Stoll had boldly predicted that the Gophers would finish the season with a winning record. Over the next four weeks, the Gophers alternated victories and losses—beating Iowa and Northwestern but losing to No. 7 Michigan and No. 1 Ohio State to take a 5-5 record into their season-finale at home against Wisconsin.

GAME OF MY LIFE

BY TONY DUNGY

Playing for Paul Bunyan's axe was the culmination of the season for us. Wisconsin had beaten us the year before, when Billy Marek had rushed for 304 yards and five touchdowns in the Badgers' 49-14 victory. I was thinking of our 15 seniors in their last home game; plus, at the time, I was one touchdown pass short of the Big Ten record.

We had a big snowstorm in Minneapolis that week, so I called my parents and told them that I didn't know whether they should come. I wasn't sure if we would even be able to play the game. Game day, though, was warm and beautiful, and the snow was piled along the sidelines.

We got off to a great start, driving right down the field; but then I threw an interception in the end zone, which cost us momentum—for a while.

Our defense kept winning the ball back for us. They had a big day in such a physical contest. They were full of fire, had something to prove.

After a scoreless first quarter, I finally threw a touchdown pass—tying the Big Ten single-season record of 13 held by Purdue's Mike Phipps—in the second quarter, hitting John Matthews just four plays after our defense had recovered a fumble at the Badgers' 33.

After that, I just kept pumping the ball to our fullback, Greg Barlow—a Madison native—who rushed for more than 100 yards. He had the fire in his eyes.

All around it was a neat day.

GAME RESULTS

Besides the touchdown pass, Dungy also rushed for two touchdowns and 85 yards and completed 6 of 14 passes for 96 yards in the Gophers' 24-3 victory, which left them with a winning record.

The Gophers defense held Marek, who had been quoted the previous year that running against the Gophers was like running against a high school team, to 118 yards and forced four turnovers by the Badgers. The Gophers outgained Wisconsin, 427-367. Led by Barlow, who gained 102 yards in 18 carries, the Gophers gained 331 yards on the ground.

The victory over the Badgers gave the Gophers a 6-5 record.

Dungy finished the season with a school-record 123 completions in 225 attempts (the 55-percent completion percentage set a school record) and a school-record 15 touchdown passes. He led the Big Ten in passing yards (1,236) and total offense (1,406) in eight conference games to become the first Gopher quarterback to lead the conference in passing. He also rushed for 244 yards and five touchdowns. Following the season, he was voted the Gophers' MVP by his teammates and elected the team captain for 1976.

Going into his senior season, Stoll said, "Dungy couldn't throw a lick as a freshman. The worst thing that happened to him was that he was the only quarterback we had when he was a sophomore. He was hurt almost all that season but we had to play him. If I had the program where it is now, I'd have red-shirted him. A lot of people gave up on Dungy after that season. But Dungy, the coaches and his teammates didn't give up on him. He made himself a great passer, and he's even better now."

"Tony's real strengths are his intangibles," Stoll told the *Chicago Tribune* in September of 1976. "He has great leadership ability. He's the brightest young man I've coached. He's an All-America man as well as an All-America athlete."

The Gophers went 6-5 again in 1976. The Gophers' 4-4 record in conference games left them tied for third place (behind co-champs Michigan and Ohio State, who were each 7-1).

The Gophers' sixth game of the 1976 season was at Michigan State—Dungy's first game at Spartan Stadium. Dungy was 7 of 9 for 133 yards in the first half and directed the Gophers' to a 14-10 victory. He was named Big Ten Back of the Week.

"That game was very meaningful," said Dungy.

For the season, Dungy completed 104 passes for 1,291 yards. He also rushed for 348 yards and five touchdowns. He graduated with six school career records and two school single-season records. He was the school's all-time leader in total offense (4,680), passing yards (3,515), attempts (586) and completions (274).

Dungy capped his college career by playing in the East/West, Hula and Japan Bowl games.

Dungy, an Academic All-American, had majored in business at the University of Minnesota.

"I had a tremendous experience at the University of Minnesota," said Dungy, an Academic All-American who majored in business. "I had internships at General Motors, Cargill and Dayton-Hudson. They were tremendous experiences. I began thinking of a job in corporate America. But like a lot of young athletes I also was thinking I wanted to be a pro football player. I figured I'd be a pro football player for six or seven years and then I would go into business."

WHAT HAPPENED TO TONY DUNGY?

Dungy signed as a free agent by the Pittsburgh Steelers in May of 1977. He made the team as a defensive back, and as a rookie in 1977 he intercepted three passes.

In 1978, he was second in the AFC with six interceptions and played in the Steelers' 35-31 victory over Dallas in Super Bowl XIII.

In 1979, he was traded to San Francisco and he played 15 games for the 49ers.

The next season he began his coaching career as a defensive backs coach at his alma mater. In 1981, he became an assistant coach for the Steelers—at 25 he was the youngest assistant in the NFL.

He spent eight seasons with the Steelers—the last four as their defensive coordinator. When he became the defensive coordinator in 1984, he was the youngest coordinator in the league. From 1989 to 1991, he was Kansas City's defensive backfield coach. From 1992-95, he was on Denny Green's Minnesota Vikings staff as the defensive coordinator.

In 1996, at the age of 40, he became the head coach of the Tampa Bay Buccaneers. He was just the fourth African American head coach (following Art Shell, Dennis Green, and Ray Rhodes) in modern NFL history.

In the 10 seasons before Dungy arrived, the Bucs were 43-111, losing 10 or more games nine times. Between 1996-2001, Dungy coached the Bucs to a 54-42 record. The Bucs, who had made only three playoff appearances in their first 20 seasons, reached the playoffs three times in six seasons under Dungy—reaching the NFC championship game following the 1999 season.

In 2002, Dungy became the Indianapolis Colts' coach. In 2005, Dungy became just the sixth coach in NFL history to win 100 regular-season games in his first 10 seasons as a NFL head coach. In 2006, the Colts won the AFC South Division title and went on to defeat the Chicago Bears, 29-17, in Super Bowl XLI.

Chapter 12

MARK CARLSON

EARLY LIFE OF MARK CARLSON

Mark Carlson said he was really lucky during his high school years at Deerfield (Illinois) High School.

"I was fortunate to play football for a good man and a good coach," said Carlson. "My coach, Paul Adams, had been a college roommate of Ray Nitschke at Illinois."

Carlson was on the Deerfield varsity three years—starting at quarterback in his junior and senior seasons.

"We lost just three games in three years," said Carlson. "My senior year, football playoffs were just getting started in Illinois. The playoffs were in their second year. We went 13-0 and won the big school (Class 5A) state championship. That really launched my exposure. It was my good fortune to play with a lot of good people and good players. It allowed me to get recruited."

After his senior season, Carlson was named a prep All-American by *Coach and Athlete Magazine* and was named one of the top two high school quarterbacks in metro Chicago by the *Chicago Tribune*. Carlson drew a lot of attention.

"Every Big Ten school but Ohio State recruited me," said Carlson. "I decided I wanted to play in the Midwest or at a Big Ten school. I wanted my family to be part of it, and I wanted my dad to be able to see me play."

NAME: Mark Stanley Carlson
BORN: October 14, 1957
POSITION: Quarterback
HEIGHT: 5-11
WEIGHT: 185
YEARS: 1977-1979
ACCOMPLISHMENTS: Team MVP
   (1979).
GAME: vs. Michigan—October
   22, 1977

Carlson, who also lettered in hockey and baseball in high school, weighed his options.

"Baseball was an influence in my decision," said Carlson. "I had met Chief (Gophers baseball coach Dick Siebert) and (Gophers football) Coach (Cal) Stoll said he would allow me to play both baseball and football.

"I was seriously considering Wisconsin, Colorado, and the U. When I was a (high school) senior, the Gophers had Tony Dungy at quarterback and threw the ball. Assistant coach Bruce Vandersall was the lead recruiter in the Chicago area. He was a tremendous guy. He built a relationship with my mom and dad. He was the difference maker in my decision."

Carlson arrived on campus in the summer of 1976, two months before school started.

"Back then school started in late September," Carlson said. "I came up early in mid-July. Coach Stoll had me room with Dungy. Tony had been involved in recruiting me. Once you got the chance to know Tony, you knew how special he was. He was my mentor. I watched him and how he went about his job. He studied so much film. He was the only player I know that the coaches made a key for to the (athletic) building so he could watch film. He probably watched more film than the coaches."

Carlson did a lot of watching and learning as a freshman.

"I was No. 2 or No. 3 on the depth chart," said Carlson, "so I traveled with the team. But I didn't play much. I was primarily a mop-up guy. I remember at Michigan, we got beat badly. I remember just going in and handing the ball off."

In his brief appearances as a freshman, Carlson didn't attempt a pass and rushed for four yards.

Mark Carlson, a native of Deerfield, Illinois, was recruited by each Big Ten school except Ohio State.

SETTING

Dungy told the *Chicago Tribune* in September of 1976 that Carlson "is going to be a lot better than me when he leaves here. He really listens and learns well. He has all the physical ability, a strong arm. He'll definitely be a good one.

Carlson had suffered a knee injury late in his freshman season that lingered into spring practice in 1977. When the Gophers started spring practice, six quarterbacks were vying to replace Dungy, who had been a three-year starter. At the start of the spring, Carlson was listed No. 3 on the depth chart (behind Wendell Avery and Marc Trestman). Avery, a sophomore, had red-shirted in 1976. In 1975, he played briefly, completing one pass for 23 yards. Trestman, a junior, had also sat out the 1976 season. Trestman had completed seven passes for 98 yards as a backup to Dungy in 1974 and 1975.

As the Gophers opened practice in the fall of 1977, Carlson was still third on the depth chart and Stoll was considering red-shirting him because of the knee injury.

"I had hurt my knee and I limped through spring practice," said Carlson. "I ended up having surgery right after spring practice. This was before arthroscopic surgery, so it was pretty invasive surgery. I spent the summer rehabbing and working back in shape. But I wasn't 100 percent as we started fall practice."

The Gophers opened the 1977 season with a 10-7 victory over Western Michigan. Avery, in his first start, was 2-for-8 for 23 yards and rushed for 58 yards.

The following week, against No. 6 Ohio State in Columbus, the Gophers played tough for three quarters—trailing by only 10 points—before falling, 38-7.

The Gophers regrouped and defeated No. 18 UCLA, 27-13. Avery passed for 60 yards but had an interception returned for a touchdown.

Against Washington, which had defeated the Gophers, 38-7, the previous season, the Gophers fell behind, 17-10, at halftime. But Paul Rogind kicked three field goals in the second half to help the Gophers rally for a 19-17 victory. Avery passed for 83 yards.

Trestman started against Northwestern in week six. Trestman completed just one pass for 10 yards but scored the Gophers' only touchdown on a two-yard run in the Gophers' 10-7 victory. Avery played the final 18½ minutes after relieving Trautman.

With Michigan coming to town, and the Gophers inconsistent on offense, Coach Stoll was considering a change at quarterback.

The top-ranked and unbeaten Wolverines presented a daunting task for the Gophers.

The Wolverines, who had rushed for 378 yards and outgained the Gophers, 418-165, in a 45-0 victory the previous season, were coming off a 56-0 victory over Wisconsin. Two weeks earlier the Wolverines had beaten No. 5 Texas A&M, 41-3. On the season, the Wolverines had outscored their six opponents, 193-42.

GAME OF MY LIFE

BY MARK CARLSON

Coach Stoll came up to me on Monday before the Michigan game and said, "If I asked you to step up and give up your redshirt year and play against Michigan, what would you say?" I didn't even blink and said, "Yes, in a heartbeat."

So, we prepared all week and I worked with the first team offense.

The night before a home game, we always stayed at the Leamington Hotel in downtown Minneapolis. We had a team meal, a team meeting, and watched a movie.

After dinner, (assistant coach) Butch Nash got up and spoke to us. As exciting as it was, as out-of-staters, we were just learning about the tradition of the Jug and the rivalry with Michigan. As 19-year - olds, we were just learning the whole tradition of the program— Bronko Nagurski, Bernie Bierman, Bruce Smith, and Murray Warmath's teams.

Butch was genuinely a passionate guy. He stood up in front of a room of 60 guys and gave a 10-minute speech about the Jug with such passion. You could hear a pin drop. I still have a picture in my home of Butch carrying the Jug off the field.

What I remember most is the way the game started. We didn't feel any pressure and we weren't intimidated by Michigan. They were ranked No. 1, but we had nothing to lose.

I think that's because we had some really good senior leadership, especially in our line. Mark Slater was our center. He went on to play in the NFL. (Left guard) Bryson Hollimon was a fifth-year senior and Desi Williamson was a senior.

We really had a tremendous team and a tremendous defense. Our linebackers—Michael Hunt, Steve Stewart, and Mark Merrill— each went on to be selected in the second round of the NFL draft. We had great upper-class leadership—Steve Midboe on defense was tough.

We came out and on the first or second play of the game, we had the ball, and I got to the line of scrimmage and looked over the defense, and called an audible—changing a run play to a pass play. I completed a 23-yard pass to Jeff Anhorn on the sideline and the crowd went crazy.

That really started us being the aggressor.

Williamson, who was a defensive end, was starting his first game at guard. On one of the first plays he came back to the huddle with his nose shattered—blood all over the place. He was screaming. He went to the sidelines and got taped up and came back in.

Marion Barber, a true freshman and just coming into his own, scored our first touchdown on an isolation play. He had a big hole and went in. Paul Rogind, my roommate for three years, kicked the extra point and three field goals.

It was exciting that Marion and Paul—who were from Michigan—were an integral part of the game.

They (Michigan) had a great offense, and our defense shut them down. We actually dominated possession time. We controlled the game. We kept it away from them and when they got the ball they were behind and had to play catch-up. They had to throw the ball and they weren't that adept at it.

We kept eating the clock and were successful kicking field goals. We had a ball-control game plan. Michigan, as they do today, played a standard, straight-up defense. They started to blitz a little, but our line was absolutely great. It created holes and protected me.

At halftime, Coach Stoll was excited. He knew we had our foot on their throat. I remember the excitement in the locker room. We wanted to go right back out there. We didn't want to waste time. We said, 'We can't let the tide turn.' Everybody was fired up. We knew we couldn't let this opportunity out of our grasp.

At the start of the second half, our defense stopped them on a three-and-out and that really helped.

When it was over, right away we had a sense of accomplishment and pride. It had been so long since we had beaten them. We went out and did it. We were not to be denied. It made us realize what we were capable of.

I remember quietly celebrating that night with my family. My dad missed only one game during my career. My (future) wife, we had met in high school, went out for dinner at the Jax Café. All of the coaches were there and we had a party.

GAME RESULTS

Carlson, making his first collegiate start and in his first extended playing time since high school, directed the Gophers to a 16-0 victory, which ended a nine-game losing streak to Michigan. The Gophers, who had been outscored by the Wolverines, 340-77, in the previous nine meetings, won the Little Brown Jug for the first time since 1967.

The Gophers, who improved to 5-2 overall and 2-2 in the Big Ten, were the first team to shut out the Wolverines in 10 years. The Wolverines hadn't been held scoreless in 112 games—a streak that dated to October 14, 1967.

Carlson's completion to Anhorn set the tone. Two plays later Carlson completed a 10-yard pass to Steve Breault for a first down at the Michigan 24. Rogind's 31-yard field goal made it 3-0.

On Michigan's first play following the ensuing kickoff, the Gophers recovered a Michigan fumble—one of five Michigan turnovers—at the Wolverines' 12. On fourth down, Barber scored the game's only touchdown on a three-yard run. Rogind converted the extra-point kick and, just seven minutes into the game, the Gophers led 10-0.

A 37-yard field goal by Rogind in the final minute of the first half gave the Gophers a 13-0 lead at the intermission.

Early in the second half, Michigan intercepted a pass and returned it to the Gophers' 8, but a pass interference penalty erased the interception. It was just one of three Michigan penalties. An interception by Ken Foxworth set up Rogind's 31-yard field goal which made it 16-0 with four minutes remaining in the game.

For the game, Carlson completed 6 of 10 passes for 60 yards. The Gophers rushed for 190 yards and outgained Michigan, 250-182. The Gophers limited the Wolverines to 80 yards rushing—125 yards below their season average. Harlan Huckleby, who was leading the Big Ten with 112 yards rushing per game, was held to 52 yards.

The Gophers stumbled after the big victory. The Gophers lost their next two—to Indiana (34-22) and to Michigan State (29-10).

"We really stubbed our toe against Indiana," said Carlson. "I didn't play very well and we didn't play with the same intensity. We gave up 34 points after shutting out Michigan."

The Gophers recovered to win their final two regular-season games—over Illinois (21-0) and Wisconsin (13-7). In the victory over Illinois, Gophers running back Kent Kitzmann carried the ball an NCAA-record 57 times for a school-record 266 yards.

Following the season the Gophers were rewarded with their first bowl game in 16 seasons. The Gophers played Maryland in the Hall of Fame Game in Birmingham, Alabama. The Terrapins won, 17-7.

"The bowl game was a great reward," said Carlson. "It was an all new experience for everybody. The game was played at Legends Field in Birmingham, where Auburn and Alabama played every year. (Alabama coach) Bear Bryant came out to one of our practices. It was a real neat time."

Interestingly, the Rose Bowl featured Michigan and Pac-10 representative Washington—two of the Gophers' seven victories in 1977. After the loss to Minnesota, the Wolverines regrouped to win their final four regular-season games (by a margin of 140-39) to secure a trip to the Rose Bowl. Washington was 1-3 after losing to the Gophers, 19-17, on October 1. The Huskies went 6-1 in conference play to earn the Rose Bowl big. The Huskies defeated the Wolverines, 27-20, in the Rose Bowl.

WHAT HAPPENED TO MARK CARLSON?

In 1978, Stoll's final season, Carlson passed for 736 yards and three touchdowns. In 1979, new coach Joe Salem and first-year offensive coordinator Mike Shanahan brought in a new offense and Carlson blossomed.

As a senior, Carlson set school records for completions, attempts, and yards as he completed 177 of 300 passes for 2,188 yards and 11 touchdowns.

"What an experience to play for Coach Salem and Coach Shanahan," said Carlson. "Coach Shanahan was 26. He was really intense. They really opened up the offense."

Following his senior season, Carlson played in the Hula Bowl, where his team was coached by Michigan's Bo Schembechler.

Carlson played baseball for the Gophers in the spring of 1980, while contemplating playing in the Canadian Football League (he had been drafted by British Columbia).

"I was really torn," said Carlson. "That spring I was healthy and enjoying baseball. We were winning the Big Ten, and it went down to the final weekend when Michigan won by percentage points. I didn't want to leave my teammates. It didn't work out. Everyone I've talked to said the CFL was a great experience. So I wish it had worked out."

In the fall of 1980, he served as a graduate assistant on Coach Salem's staff.

In the spring of 1981, he gave up his senior year of baseball eligibility to play for a Chicago team in a first-year pro football league (the American Football Association League). He completed 60 percent of his passes and led his team to the league championship game.

In early 1981 Carlson and his wife became parents. Their son, Kevin, went on to be a four-year letterman for the Gophers baseball team.

Chapter 13

MARION BARBER

EARLY LIFE OF MARION BARBER

As one of the top high school running backs in Michigan, there was a lot of pressure on Marion Barber of Detroit Chadsey High School to play football for the nearby University of Michigan. Including some not-so-subtle pressure from the University of Michigan coach.

"When I was a high school senior," said Barber, "(Michigan coach) Bo Schembechler was in our locker room after a basketball game. We sat on a bench about a foot apart. He said to me, 'You owe it to the state of Michigan (to play for the Wolverines).' I was kind of intimidated by that. I suppose he said that to every recruit in the state. But I was thinking, 'Nope, that's not where I want to go.'"

Barber had his sights set on another U. of M. and he was going to have to convince his mother.

"My mom wanted me to stay close to home," said Barber. "She told me she'd buy me a car if I stayed home. I knew a lot of guys attending Michigan, guys like Harlan Huckleby, Gordon Bell, and Tom Seabron, but I decided to visit Minnesota."

Gophers coach Cal Stoll, who had been assistant to Michigan State coach Duffy Daugherty for 10 years, recruited the state of Michigan well. Several years earlier, Stoll had lured quarterback Tony Dungy from Michigan.

NAME: Marion Sylvester Barber
BORN: December 6, 1959
POSITION: Running back
HEIGHT: 6-3
WEIGHT: 224
YEARS: 1977-1980
ACCOMPLISHMENTS: First team All-Big Ten (1978, 1980).
GAME: vs. Indiana—November 4, 1978

Barber said the recruiting trip to the Minnesota was enjoyable.

"I had a good time in Minnesota," said Barber. "I remember the barn (Williams Arena). The atmosphere was unreal. We went out for dinner, and I remember seeing a couple of the Vikings—Ahmad Rashad and Sammy White. I was thinking, 'Did they stage that for me?' I loved Minnesota hockey. Olympia Stadium was not far from where I grew up and I remember seeing the Gophers play a game there. I knew (Gophers wide receiver) Mike Jones. And, my mother had been in contact with Tony Dungy's mother. So I knew bits and pieces about Minnesota and had some ties."

When he returned to Detroit from his recruiting visit, Barber told his stepfather, who was in the hospital being treated for cancer, that Minnesota was where he wanted to go.

"He said, 'If that's where you want to go, that's where you should go. Your mother will be alright.' He passed a week after my trip to Minnesota."

The University of Minnesota offered independence, but Barber said it was also a "Big Ten school close enough to home so that I could get home if I had to."

Years later, Barber told the *Minneapolis Star Tribune*, "I guess I wanted to more or less declare my independence. Minnesota for me was just the best opportunity to fulfill the dreams I had."

When the Gophers started fall practice in 1977, Barber was one of seven freshmen among the 16 running backs on the Gophers' roster competing for playing time. The 6-foot-3, 210-pound Barber quickly asserted himself and found himself in the starting lineup.

One of 16 running backs on the Gophers roster, Marion Barber quickly moved into the starting lineup as a freshman.

In his Gophers debut, Barber rushed 10 times for 41 yards in the Gophers' 10-7 victory over Western Michigan. The 1977 season would include several more highlights for Barber and the Gophers.

On October 22, the Gophers stunned top-ranked Michigan, 16-0. Barber scored the Gophers' lone touchdown, and Michigan native Paul Rogind kicked three field goals for the Gophers. After the game, Schembechler wouldn't acknowledge Barber or let any of the Wolverines speak to him.

In the Gophers' next-to-last regular-season game, running back Kent Kitzmann carried the ball an NCAA-record 57 times for 266 yards in the Gophers' 21-0 victory over Illinois. That victory made the Gophers bowl eligible. The next week, the Gophers defeated Wisconsin, 13-7, to improve to 7-4.

The Gophers were rewarded with their first bowl invitation since the 1961 season and played Maryland in the Hall of Fame Bowl in Birmingham, Alabama. The Gophers, the first Big Ten team other than Michigan or Ohio State to play in a bowl game since 1972, lost to the Terrapins, 17-7. Barber scored the Gophers' lone touchdown. For the season, Barber finished with 582 yards in 128 carries—an average of 4.5 yards per carry.

Barber's workload increased in his sophomore season. But that wasn't the only change coming. The 1978 season would be the seventh and final season as Gophers coach for Stoll.

The Gophers opened the season with a 38-12 victory over Toledo before 31,223 at Memorial Stadium. But they lost their next three games—No. 16 Ohio State (27-10), UCLA (17-3) and Oregon State (17-14)—to fall to 1-3. The Gophers evened their record with victories over Iowa (22-20) and Northwestern (38-14), but the following week, they lost at No. 8 Michigan, 42-10, to fall to 3-4.

As the Gophers prepared for their next game—homecoming against Indiana—speculation in the media about Stoll's job security started.

In his six-plus seasons as coach, heading into the Indiana game, Stoll had directed the Gophers to a 37-37 overall record and a 25-26 record in Big Ten games—the fourth-best record in the Big Ten during that time.

But Stoll's record against the Big Ten Conference's Big Two—Ohio State and Michigan—was the primary source of dissatisfaction. Those two teams were in the midst of a 12-year stretch where they dominated the conference. Between 1969-1981, Ohio State (seven times) and Michigan (six times) were the only Big Ten teams to play in the Rose Bowl). The loss to Michigan the previous week gave Stoll a 1-13 record against the Big Two.

Indiana, coached by Lee Corso, also brought a 3-4 record into the game. The Hoosiers had won two of their previous three games going into the Gophers game.

The Hoosiers had won three of the previous four meetings between the two teams. In 1977, the Gophers were ranked No. 19—their first appearance in the Top 25 since the first week of the 1969 season—going into the game at Indiana. The Hoosiers won, 34-22. The loss dropped the Gophers out of the poll and they wouldn't return to the Top 25 until 1985.

GAME OF MY LIFE

BY MARION BARBER

When it first came up, I think (people assume) the Michigan game from my freshman year would be my most memorable game. Probably, because I was from Michigan and because it was against the Wolverines. There was a lot to remember about my freshman year. We went to a bowl game. Beating both Michigan and Washington, and they both went to the Rose Bowl. We beat UCLA.

But for me, it was the Indiana game, my sophomore year. It was homecoming. I remember riding down University Avenue in a car (in the homecoming parade). I can't remember the themes of the other homecoming games while I was at the University, but I can remember the theme from this one—the Roaring Twenties.

And, the way the game started out, who thought we'd come back to win?

We were down, 24-7, at halftime, but we had players like Wendell Avery come through for us. Wendell came off the bench in the fourth quarter and led us on three scoring drives.

There were just so many things that had to go right for us, after we fell behind. The offense and the defense and special teams all played well. Wendell engineered the winning drive. Keith Edwards had a couple of interceptions for us.

The other thing that really stands out from that day is the people. Even after we fell behind, they (a Memorial Stadium crowd of 39,797) stuck around. I think about that now because if you go to a game now, and a team gets behind, the fans leave early.

It's not like we were getting outplayed that day. We had made a bunch of mistakes and committed some turnovers. Everything we did seemed to turn out wrong. We were moving the ball all over the place and then we'd make a turnover that would kill us.

I fumbled on the sideline inside the 10-yard line and it got picked up and returned 92 yards (by Dale Kneipp) for a touchdown. I couldn't believe what was happening.

At halftime Coach Stoll was always enthusiastic and was a motivator. Whatever he thought the mood was, he would flow with it. He told us things like that (the fumble) happen during a game. He said we needed to stop doing that (turnovers) and play the way he knew we could. That was the gist of his talk at halftime.

But we came out in the second half, and still didn't quite get it right. But suddenly things started falling into place.

We completed consecutive screen passes, which is unusual because usually once you complete one, the other team is able to adjust. We were successful on a two-point conversion. Wendell almost got sacked, and then he hit for two. Paul Rogind. Keith Edwards. The list goes on. They all had big games.

It was really a team effort.

As a sophomore in 1978, Marion Barber became just the second Gopher to rush for more than 1,000 yards in a season.

GAME RESULTS

Rogind's 31-yard field goal with five seconds remaining lifted the Gophers to a 32-31 victory.

Kneipp's fumble return—which is still an Indiana school record—gave the Hoosiers a 17-0 lead as they built a 24-0 lead late in the first half. Barber's one-yard touchdown run got the Gophers on the scoreboard with two and a half minutes remaining in the half.

The Gophers, who had gained 320 yards and 16 first downs in the first half, started the second half with two more turnovers before Barber scored again—on a two-yard run— late in the third quarter to pull the Gophers within 24-14. But the Hoosiers scored early in the fourth quarter to extend their lead to 31-14.

The Gophers' comeback started when Avery, who hadn't been expected to play because of bruised ribs, threw a 14-yard touchdown pass (on a screen play) to Roy Artis. The extra-point kick made it 31-21 with nine-plus minutes remaining.

On the ensuing possession, the Gophers forced Indiana to punt, and Avery drove the Gophers 56 yards in 10 plays. The drive culminated in Avery's 19-yard screen pass to Barber for a touchdown. Avery then hit Elmer Bailey for the two-point conversion to make it 31-29 with 4:06 remaining.

Edwards' interception—his third of the game—gave the Gophers the ball at the Indiana with two and a half minutes remaining. The Gophers drove 45 yards in nine plays to set up Rogind's game-winning field goal.

Barber, who had a fourth touchdown called back because of a penalty, rushed for 177 yards and caught four passes for 36 yards as the Gophers amassed 577 yards in offense. The Gophers overcame seven turnovers and seven penalties.

The Gophers lost at Michigan State, 33-9, the next week but defeated Illinois, 24-6, on senior day. Barber keyed that victory by rushing for 233 yards in 36 carries. The big day left Barber with

1,099 yards on the season and made him just the second runner in school history to reach that plateau (John King rushed for 1,164 yards 1972—Stoll's first season as Gophers coach).

The Gophers took a 5-5 record into the regular-season finale against Wisconsin, and the game was considered a must win for Stoll's job security. The Badgers romped past the Gophers, 48-10. Following the season, Stoll, who signed a contract extension in 1977, was fired with two years remaining on his contract. The Gophers were 39-39 in seven seasons under Stoll.

Barber, who rushed for 111 yards against the Badgers to finish the season with a school-record 1,210 yards, was named first team All-Big Ten.

Stoll was replaced by Joe Salem, a former Gophers quarterback who was a member of the Gophers' 1960 national championship team. Salem brought in a run-and-shoot offense, which decreased Barber's workload.

As a junior in 1979, Barber averaged 4.1 yards per carry as he gained 526 yards in 127 carries (120 carries fewer than the previous season). He rushed for 12 touchdowns.

The Gophers, who were 4-3 after defeating the Iowa Hawkeyes, 24-7, went 0-3-1 in the final four games to finish with a 4-6-1 record.

Barber's senior season was hampered by an injury, which forced him to miss three games. But he still averaged a career-best 5.0 yards per carry as he gained 769 yards in 154 carries. He scored 11 touchdowns.

The Gophers had started the season with just two victories in their first six games. But a three-game winning streak left them with a 5-4 record with two games remaining. Losses to Michigan State and Wisconsin left them 5-6.

Barber, who had 12 100-yard rushing games in his career, finished with 3,094 yards and 34 touchdowns—both school records at the time.

WHAT HAPPENED TO MARION BARBER?

Barber went into the 1981 draft ranked as the third-best fullback prospect. The New York Jets selected him in the second round—the 30th player selected overall.

Barber's professional career almost never got started. Early in his first training camp, he suffered a concussion. He was placed on injured reserve and missed the entire season. Although he missed the entire 1981 season—he was able to return to practice late in the season.

He went into training camp in 1982, listed fourth (out of four) on the Jets' depth chart at fullback. When he gained just 14 yards in six carries in the Jets' first two preseason games, it appeared he would be cut.

But Barber made the team and went on to play seven seasons for the Jets. During his career, Barber was primarily used as a special teams player and a blocking fullback.

Barber had returned to school after the 1981 season to finish his degree and was married in June of 1982. He and his wife, Karen, have three sons.

Sons Marion III and Dominique followed in their father's path to play football for Minnesota. Marion III surpassed his father's rushing totals for the Gophers and was fourth on the Gophers' all-time rushing list (3,276 yards) after the 2006 season. Marion Barber, who held the school career rushing record for eight years before Darrell Thompson broke the record as a junior in 1988, is currently sixth on the all-time list.

Dominique Barber, a defensive back, was a junior with the Gophers in 2006. Barber said having his sons play for the Gophers has been special.

"For me it's a warm fuzzy (feeling)," said Barber, "that they felt strongly about playing for the U and a love and desire to try and help the Gophers. I can't help but be excited."

Barber, who works in the food wholesale business, said he has always tried to be there for his sons after one of their games.

"I understand what they're going through as a player," said Barber. "It's tough to come out of the locker room after a loss. I've always tried to be the same—win or lose. They need a calm after the storm."

Chapter 14

MIKE HOHENSEE

EARLY LIFE OF MIKE HOHENSEE

Maybe growing up with four siblings in a crowded house in Southern California prepared Mike Hohensee for working for a competitive guy like Mike Ditka.

"We lived in a three-bedroom house," said Hohensee, "so you can only imagine how close we were with seven people living in such a small house. We were very competitive as kids. Everything was a contest, including chores . . . whose was cleanest or who finished first."

As a youth in Rowland Heights, Hohensee played baseball and basketball and he started playing football when he was eight years old.

"I grew up playing on the beach or going to the park and competing against kids from all over California," said Hohensee. "Competition drove me. As a youth, I played in a very high-level program."

But Hohensee's high school (Rowland) football team was average.

"We were not very good," said Hohensee. "I hated losing. I felt like a fish out of water. I couldn't understand why other guys didn't want to be great at something. I was known as a great punter and a diamond in the rough as a quarterback."

Following his senior season, Hohensee played in the San Gabriel Valley All-Star football game.

"I was fortunate enough to play (in the all-star game)," said Hohensee. "The star quarterback was injured and I came in and won the MVP award."

Hohensee, who hadn't received a scholarship offer from any major college football program, enrolled at Mt. San College (Mt. SAC) in nearby Walnut, California.

Hohensee began the 1979 season sharing the quarterback duties, but he eventually won the starting job. Hohensee led Mt. SAC to a 7-2 record by passing for 2,112 yards and 13 touchdowns. Hohensee was just the fifth quarterback in South Coast Conference history to pass for more than 2,000 yards.

But the season had its ups and downs for Hohensee.

"I almost left school my first season," said Hohensee. "I didn't like the way the coach addressed the players and I felt I had enough. Coach Russell, our receivers coach, came and talked me out of it."

As a sophomore, Hohensee led Mt. SAC to its first conference title in 26 years. In one game that season, Hohnesse set a conference record by passing for 492 yards and tied a conference-record with five touchdown passes in a victory over San Diego Messa in San Diego. Hohensee finished the season leading the conference in

---

NAME: Michael Louis Hohensee
BORN: February 22, 1961
POSITION: Quarterback
HEIGHT: 6-0
WEIGHT: 205
YEARS: 1981-1982
ACCOMPLISHMENTS: Two-time
  team MVP.
GAME: vs. Ohio State—
  November 7, 1981

Coming out of high school, Mike Hohensee did not receive a scholarship offer from any major college program. After two years at a California junior college, Hohensee chose the Gophers over Wisconsin.

138

passing (1,761 yards) and total offense (1,976 yards) and was named the conference's offensive player of the year.

Even after two outstanding seasons in a very competitive conference, Hohensee was not highly recruited.

"I was briefly recruited by Wisconsin and Cal State Fullerton," said Hohensee. "(Coach) Steve Mariucci was the (Cal State Fullerton) assistant coach who took me out to lunch at a Sizzler. He told me to order anything I wanted. He was just a young man himself at the time. They (Cal State Fullerton) were in the process of rebuilding their program."

SETTING

One more school had taken an interest in Hohensee.

"Minnesota came into the picture late," said Hohensee. "They were actually looking at one of my teammates and saw me play in my last game. I went on my first airplane ride for my recruiting trip to Minnesota. I was your typical jock. I didn't go to any parties in high school. So all the hoopla that occurs for recruits was new to me. I was picked up at the airport by (assistant coach) Tony Dungy, who at the time I knew nothing about."

Joe Salem, who has just completed his second season as the Gophers coach, was looking for depth at the quarterback position.

"My son (Tim) had started at quarterback for us (the previous season) as a freshman," said Salem. "Playing in the Big Ten as a freshman is tough. At the end of the year, he had some injuries, so were just looking for some help."

After his visit, Hohensee picked Minnesota.

"I had a good meeting with Coach Salem," said Hohensee, "and, I felt I could start based on who they had at the time. Coach Salem assured me that even though his son Tim was the current starter I would be given every chance to win the job. I trusted him. I had a gut feeling about him."

Hohensee arrived on campus in time for spring football in 1981.

"I remember arriving while everyone was on spring break," said Hohensee. "I was there for a week by myself and I was homesick. I

140

was in an empty dorm and this was my first time away from home. It was rough for awhile. College was different in so many ways and it had nothing to do with football."

Hohensee began spring practice low on the Gophers' depth chart.

"I started off spring ball sixth on the depth chart," said Hohensee, "which would play with a lot of guys' minds, but I grew up with my dad doing things like that to me all the time. I just figured it was my job to take. There was nowhere to go, but up."

By the end of spring practice, Hohensee had moved up to No. 2 on the depth chart.

"That's how it stayed through the summer," said Hohensee. "I went home determined to win the job in the fall. I came back in the best shape of my life."

After the first two weeks of fall practice, Hohensee hadn't won the starting job. A week before the Gophers' season-opener (September 12 vs. Ohio U.), Coach Salem still hadn't announced his starting quarterback.

"I didn't find out I won the job until the week of the first game," said Hohensee. "I was lifting in the morning and heard it on the radio that I was starting. I was surprised. I thought since I hadn't heard anything yet that Tim was going to start. I was thrilled of course."

The Gophers and Hohensee got off to a good start—winning their first three games.

THE GAME OF MY LIFE

BY MIKE HOHENSEE

There was a lot of excitement around the U. We were playing well. We had opened the season with a 19-17 victory over Ohio University. The next week, we upset Purdue, 16-13. In week three, against Oregon State, I threw (a school-record) five touchdown passes and we were just playing good football.

In his fourth start for the Gophers, Mike Hohensee set three school records as he led the Gophers to their first victory over Ohio State in 13 games.

Then came Ohio State. All I heard was that we hadn't beaten them in 15 years. That's all I needed to hear to create some sort of challenge to myself.

That week I watched more film than I had ever watched before. I remember the exact time I thought I knew we were going to win. I was watching film with (receiver) Chester Cooper and saw a sure give away by one of their defensive backs that gave away the coverage they would play. I showed Chester and he flashed that big smile and just looked at me in agreement.

It was a hard-fought game by both teams. We were behind almost the whole game, but there was a calm in our huddle that overrode any thoughts of not winning. We were so well prepared that we just knew our time had come. We used so many different formations that we kept them off guard. They were throwing the defensive book at us but we always had an answer—a great run, a great catch, a great defensive stand, or a great call.

We had a great game plan. Jay (Carroll) kept on coming back and telling me he was open and I was able to hit him on those (three) touchdown passes.

We knew we could pass. But we thought maybe 30-40 times. Not 67. We always had somebody open. When they gave us something, we took it. When they stopped that, they always gave us something else. We always knew when the blitz was coming.

This was my finest day as a collegiate player, yes; but I feel it was Coach Salem's finest as a coach. That day Ohio State was outplayed, yes; but they were also outcoached.

One side note was the players that had been there before me were constantly talking about they had seen (Ohio State quarterback and Heisman Trophy candidate) Art (Schlichter) come back so many times before and to not let down.

I'm glad we won for all those guys before me and for those who grew up in Minnesota and endured all of those previous losses.

Thank you for taking me back. I have (had) a continual smile on my face thinking of all the people who touched my life in that wonderfully awkward time of my life. I have a gut feeling many more wonderful experiences will come my way. Trust your gut.

GAME RESULTS

At the end of the three-hour, 29-minute marathon, Hohensee had set three school records in the Gophers' 35-31 come-from-behind victory over the Buckeyes.

Hohensee had completed 37 of 67 passes for 444 yards as the Gophers rallied from 14-0, 21-7 and 31-21 deficits.

The Gophers, who trailed 21-7 at halftime, still trailed by 10 points (31-21) with seven minutes remaining. Hohensee's 18-yard touchdown pass to Jay Carroll with 6:56 remaining pulled the Gophers within 31-27. The game-winning touchdown—a 28-yarder to Carroll—came with 2:38 remaining.

Hohensee's favorite target was Cooper, who caught 12 passes for a school-record 182 yards. Fullback Ron Jacobs caught nine passes (64 yards, one touchdown) and end Ron Weckbacker caught eight passes for 93 yards.

Carroll was the hero—turning each of his three receptions into a touchdown.

The loss dropped the Buckeyes, who were ranked No. 18, out of first place in the Big Ten standings and into a tie for third place. The Buckeyes fell to 6-3 overall and 4-2 in the conference. The Gophers improved to 6-3 overall and 4-3 in the conference.

But the momentum from the victory didn't last. One week later in East Lansing, Michigan, the Gophers were outscored by Michigan State, 43-36.

In their regular-season finale—and their final game in Memorial Stadium—the Gophers lost to Wisconsin, 26-21. Both teams went into the game with a 6-4 record, and the loss dropped the Gophers to sixth place in the Big Ten standings and ended any bowl hopes. The Badgers went on to play in the Garden State Bowl—their first bowl appearance since the 1963 Rose Bowl.

A new era for Gopher football began in 1982 as they moved off campus to the Metrodome. The Gophers opened the season with a 57-3 victory over Ohio University before 56,168 at the Metrodome. The Gophers followed up with victories at Purdue (36-10) and over Washington State (41-11) to improve to 3-0 and move into the AP

Top 25 rankings for the first time in 13 years. In the victory over Washington State, Hohensee threw two touchdown passes to set a school record of 26 (in just 14 games). Hohensee broke the record of 25, held by Tony Dungy.

In the fourth week of the 1982 season, the Gophers played host to Illinois in front of a national TV audience (CBS) and a near-sellout crowd of 63,684.

Illinois dominated the second half en route to a 42-24 victory over the Gophers. The following week, the Gophers lost at Northwestern, 31-21. The Gophers lost their final six games to finish the season with a 3-8 record.

Hohensee finished his two-year Gopher career with at least six school passing records—completions (392), attempts (722), interceptions (31), yards (4,792), yards per game (217.8) and touchdowns (33).

Following the season, Hohensee was invited to play in the Hula Bowl in Hawaii. On January 15, 1983, Hohensee and teammates Curt Warner (Penn State) and Dan Marino (Pittsburgh) led the East to a 30-14 victory over the West. Hohensee completed four of six passes for 93 yards and threw a 43-yard touchdown pass to Notre Dame's Tony Hunter to make it 17-0 in the second quarter. Marino, who passed for 156 yards, was named the offensive player of the game.

WHAT HAPPENED TO MIKE HOHENSEE?

Hohensee was the 50th player selected in the USFL draft in 1983 and spent two years with the Washington Generals. Hohensee played in the CFL in 1985 and 1986. In 1987, he was out of football and working at a factory when he got asked to play for Pittsburgh of the first-year Arena League (AFL). He threw the first touchdown pass in AFL history (in June of 1987) and in one game in 1988 passed for nine touchdowns. In the fall of 1987, Hohensee appeared in two games for the Chicago Bears.

In 1989, Hohensee began his coaching career as an assistant coach for the Chicago Bruisers of the Arena League. He became the youngest head coach in the AFL when he took over the Washington Commandos in 1990. He coached three other Arena League teams before becoming the coach of the expansion Chicago Rush in September of 2000.

In 2006, Hohensee directed the Rush—owned by former Chicago Bears coach Mike Ditka—to the AFL title. The 2006 season was Hohensee's 20th season in the AFL.

"I'm having a blast," said Hohensee. "We just won the world championship. We did it the hard way. We started out 4-8, won our last two regular-season games to qualify for the playoffs, and won four in a row on the road to win the Arena bowl. After we won the first round I had a gut feeling we would win it all. I played in the first one in 1987 and didn't get back into the championship again for 20 years."

Chapter 15

RICKEY FOGGIE

EARLY LIFE OF RICKEY FOGGIE

Mattie Pearl Foggie always knew where her youngest child was. If Rickey Foggie wasn't in the house, she knew he was nearby.

"Rickey was always playing ball. If he wasn't at home, I knew he was (over) playing ball," Mattie Pearl Foggie told the *Minneapolis Star Tribune.* "Morning, noon and night. But even if it hadn't been for it, I know he would have never gotten into any kind of trouble. I just don't let my children get into trouble."

"I was the baby of nine kids," said Rickey Foggie. "I had four brothers and four sisters. All of my siblings were involved in sports. So I grew up around sports. I was either watching my siblings or playing sports in the backyard."

Rickey Foggie grew up to be a four-sport standout at Laurens (S.C.) High School—10 miles from his hometown of Waterloo, South Carolina.

In baseball, Foggie was an all-conference pitcher. In football, he helped Laurens win the South Carolina Class AAAA Division II state title in 1983. In basketball, he was All-State and in track he high-jumped 6-foot-6.

Rickey's father, Willie, thought his youngest son would play baseball in college.

"I always figured he was going to play baseball," Willie Foggie told the *Minneapolis Star Tribune.* "He must have only been seven or eight when he started playing. But he loved all sports."

Rickey Foggie, who began playing quarterback as a high school junior, began getting attention for his football ability.

NAME: Rickey Foggie
BORN: July 15, 1966
POSITION: Quarterback
HEIGHT: 6-2
WEIGHT: 195
YEARS: 1984-1987
ACCOMPLISHMENTS: Second team All-Big Ten (1987); Bronko Nagurski Award winner (1984, 1985, 1987); UM Athletic Hall of Fame.
GAME: vs. Clemson (Independence Bowl)—December 21, 1985

"We had a tailback named Leonard Pulley, who rushed for 2,100 yards and 35 touchdowns," Rickey Foggie said. "I got noticed when coaches came around to look at Leonard."

One coach who noticed Foggie was an East Carolina assistant coach.

"Coach (John) Palermo came to watch our tailback and he noticed me," said Rickey Foggie. "I had good grades and a good SAT score, so East Carolina was interested in me. But, then, all of a sudden, Coach Palermo had been hired at Minnesota."

Palermo had joined the staff of new Gophers coach Lou Holtz as a defensive line coach. Foggie weighed the interest of the Gophers and a third school—North Carolina. Foggie was looking for an opportunity to play quarterback in college.

"North Carolina told me they would move me around from wide receiver, to running back, to defensive back," said Foggie. "I was okay with that, because I had played all those positions up until

---

Rickey Foggie was just the third freshman to start at quarterback for head coach Lou Holtz.

my junior year. Coach Palermo said I'd get a fair shot (at Minnesota) to play quarterback. I said, 'Alright, that's cool.' My parents left it up to me. I felt comfortable with Coach Palermo."

Foggie's mother told the *Minneapolis Star Tribune,* "At first I wanted him to stay closer to home. He's my baby. But he makes friends and we thought he should make up his own mind. He's very determined person."

Foggie decided to go to school nearly 1,200 miles from home.

"My parents drove up to Minnesota from South Carolina," said Foggie. "I remember my mother telling me, when they dropped me off, 'We'll come to visit you. But we're not coming back here to bring you home.'"

SETTING

When Foggie reported for practice in the fall of 1984, he recalled, "I was No. 5 on the depth chart at quarterback. They moved me from running back, to wide receiver, to punt returner. I muffed the first punt I handled and Coach Holtz yelled, 'Get out of there.'"

Holtz expected returning letterman Brett Sadek to be the Gophers starter at quarterback and highly recruited freshman Dan Ford, an All-State quarterback from Tulsa, to be his backup.

"The first week of practice we were running a pass/power-I offense," said Foggie. "In the second week we started incorporating an option offense exactly like I had run in high school."

Foggie quickly moved up the depth chart, but Holtz, who was beginning his 15th season as a college head coach, rarely rushed freshmen into action.

"I've only had two other freshmen start for me at quarterback," Holtz told the *Minneapolis Star Tribune.* "I'd rather not have to play any freshmen. I'd rather let them learn the system and get their feet on the ground in school."

Foggie made a spectacular debut in the Gophers' season-opener against Rice, when he came off the bench to throw a touchdown pass and rush for 50 yards in the Gophers' 31-24 victory over the Owls. The following week the Gophers lost to No. 1 Nebraska, 38-7, and when the Gophers' offense was ineffective in the first half against Purdue the next week, Foggie was inserted into the lineup.

"It was exciting," Foggie said. "But I didn't feel any pressure. My mom and my dad had always instilled in me 'to go out and do your best, give 100 percent and let the chips fall.' I knew the game plan, the plays and could read defenses. Coach (offensive coordinator Larry) Beckish and Coach Holtz had me so well prepared, I didn't feel any pressure."

Foggie made his first start the following week in a 35-22 loss to No. 3 Ohio State.

The loss to Ohio State dropped the Gophers to 1-3, but with Foggie in the starting lineup the Gophers won three of their final seven games to finish with a 4-7 record. The Gophers concluded the season with a 23-17 victory over Iowa. For the season, Foggie rushed for 647 yards and passed for 1,036 yards and 10 touchdowns. Realizing that Foggie was the quarterback of the future for the Gophers, Sadek and Ford both transferred after the season.

"We won four games that year and I don't think a lot of people expected us to win four," said Foggie. "I think Wisconsin had 11 players drafted from that team. A lot of Big Ten teams didn't know how to play defense against an option. That helped us be competitive."

The Gophers opened the 1985 season with a 28-14 victory over Wichita State and a 62-17 victory over Montana. The 62 points in the victory over the Grizzlies were the most by the Gophers in 46 years (the Gophers opened the 1939 season with a 62-0 victory over Arizona).

The week after beating Montana, the Gophers played host to No. 3 Oklahoma. The Sooners, and quarterback Troy Aikman, outlasted the Gophers, 13-7.

Foggie and the Gophers rebounded with three consecutive victories—at home against Purdue (45-15) and on the road at Northwestern (21-10) and Indiana (22-7)—to improve to 5-1. The back-to-back conference road victories were rare for the Gophers, who had gone 3-14 on the road in the Big Ten between 1981-1984.

At the end of his Gophers career in 1987, Rickey Foggie was just one of three players in college football history to have passed for 4,000 yards and rushed for 2,000 yards.

The victory over Indiana also earned the Gophers a spot in the Associated Press Top 20 (at No. 20) for the first time since the fourth week of the 1982 season. The Gophers fell short against No. 9 Ohio State, 23-19, before a sellout crowd at the Metrodome.

The Gophers suffered another tough loss the next week at Michigan State—31-26—but they defeated Wisconsin, 27-18, in the sold-out Metrodome for their sixth victory of the season. The Gophers concluded the regular season with losses to two Top 10 teams—No. 8 Michigan and No. 3 Iowa.

The Gophers accepted a bid to play Clemson in the Independence Bowl, but Holtz wouldn't be leading them. Less than a week after the loss to Iowa, Holtz accepted an offer from Notre Dame to become the coach of the Fighting Irish. Gophers defensive coordinator John Gutekunst, who had never been a head college coach, was named the interim head coach and would lead the Gophers in the bowl game.

GAME OF MY LIFE

BY RICKEY FOGGIE

I was disappointed and surprised when Coach Holtz left for Notre Dame. I remember my high school coach warned me. He said, "Coach Holtz will come in and fix the program and then leave.' I said, "No, he's staying."

If you look at where the program was in 1983, it was a doormat. Coach Holtz instilled a lot of confidence in us. We'd run through a wall for him. He always had us prepared. He covered everything. On Thursdays, we'd have a walk-through practice and he'd have us like down in the grass. He'd have 80-90 guys on the ground visualizing positive images.

No question we were happy for the juniors and seniors who had been there in 1982 and 1983. Those guys set precedents for us and were leaders. They were so hungry for wins. The games were easier than Coach Holtz's practices. The juniors and seniors worked so hard—they wanted to get out of that rut of losing so bad.

We had confidence in Coach Gutekunst. He was the opposite of Coach Holtz. He was laid back and he got along with the players. Coach Gutekunst and Coach Beckish kept us focused and got us ready for the bowl game.

It definitely was a memorable game for me. My childhood hero had been (Clemson quarterback) Homer Jordan. Clemson was only 45 minutes to an hour away from my hometown. I watched them every weekend on TV. Jordan led them to the national championship in 1981.

I was disappointed I never got recruited by Clemson. The word I got from my high school coach was they thought I was too slow. There's no doubt they didn't think I was experienced enough at quarterback. I was disappointed I didn't get to play for them, but I was more disappointed I didn't get recruited by them.

I knew some of the guys on the team. I had played against quarterback Rodney Williams in high school.

It was great for me. My parents were able to drive to Shreveport for the game. My mom only saw me play a couple other games during my career. With nine kids, we didn't have a lot of money. So it was special.

In the first half, our defense played great and forced three turnovers. I remember hitting Mel Anderson with a touchdown pass. In the fourth quarter we were able to make some plays and put together two long scoring drives.

There's no question, it was a big win for our seniors. It was such a close-knit group. I remember guys like Pete Najarian and David Puk running to the sidelines at the end of the game with these great looks on their faces. Their faces told the story. We (the underclassmen) figured we'd go back to another bowl game, so it was a great win for the seniors.

It was really fun to be part of the bowl game. When we started the season 5-1, the city and the university really got behind us. It was a great atmosphere that season, playing in front of the sold-out crowds in the dome and the whole aura.

GAME RESULTS

Foggie directed the Gophers on two fourth-quarter scoring drives to help the Gophers rally for a 20-13 victory over Clemson.

The Gophers led 10-6 at halftime, but Clemson had a 13-10 lead after three quarters.

Foggie rushed three times for 30 yards and also completed a 22-yard pass to tight end Craig Otto on third-and-11 to set up Chip Lohmiller's 19-yard field goal, which tied the score with 10:45 remaining.

On the Gophers' next possession, Foggie completed passes of 10 and 14 yards to fuel a scoring drive, which was capped by Valdez Baylor's one-yard touchdown, which put the Gophers ahead 19-13 with 4:56 remaining.

For the game, Foggie finished with 60 yards rushing (in 18 carries) and completed 9 of 21 passes for 123 yards. Foggie's nine-yard touchdown pass to Mel Anderson—which capped a 91-yard scoring drive—gave the Gophers a 9-0 lead in the second quarter. Clemson, which was making its first bowl appearance in four years, turned the ball over on each of its first three possessions.

The Gophers finished the season with a 7-5 record—their first winning season since the 1977 season.

The highlight of the 1986 regular season for Foggie and the Gophers was a 20-17 victory over No. 2 Michigan in Ann Arbor. Foggie set up Chip Lohmiller's game-winning 30-yard field goal as time expired with a 31-yard scramble to the Michigan 17-yard line. Following a 30-27 loss to Iowa in their regular-season finale, the Gophers played Tennessee in the Liberty Bowl in Memphis.

Tennessee used a fourth-quarter touchdown to break a tie and outlast the Gophers, who were making a back-to-back appearance in a bowl for the first time since the 1961 and 1962 Rose Bowls, 21-14. Foggie rushed for 52 yards and completed 10 passes for 136 yards. Foggie's 11-yard touchdown run in the third quarter pulled the Gophers within 14-9.

Foggie's senior season was delayed when he sat out the Gophers' first two games. The Gophers won those two games and won their next three for their first 5-0 start to a season since the national championship season of 1960. But the Gophers lost five of their final six games—including a 34-20 loss at Iowa in the regular-season finale—and did not earn a third consecutive bowl-game bid.

The lone victory in the Gophers' final six games in 1987 was a 22-19 come-from-behind victory over Wisconsin, when Foggie completed 5-of-5 passes for 42 yards and threw the game-winning touchdown pass in the final two minutes.

Foggie told the *Minneapolis Star Tribune*:

> "When I look back on my career, I'll have a lot of good memories. I had a good time here. I got a chance to play quarterback, the position I wanted to play at a major college. But the one thing that's disappointing is I just think our record could have been better. When you're the quarterback, you take it upon yourself to take the blame when you come up short."

WHAT HAPPENED TO RICKEY FOGGIE?

Following his senior season, Foggie was named by his teammates as the team's MVP for the third time in four seasons. Foggie, who was second in the Big Ten in total offense in his senior season, finished his Gophers career with a school-record 5,162 yards passing and 2,150 rushing yards (sixth best in school history) for a school-record 7,312 yards in total offense.

At the time he was one of just three players in college football history to pass for 4,000 yards and rush for 2,000 yards.

"I hate to see him go," Gophers coach John Gutekunst told the *Minneapolis Star Tribune*. "I'm gonna miss the smile he always has on his face. And when I look back in a few years, I'll think of him as one of the truly outstanding all-purpose quarterbacks."

Despite the numbers, Foggie was not drafted by an NFL team. But Foggie still managed to have a long and productive career in professional football.

He began his pro football career in Canada. During his eight seasons in Canada, Foggie played on two Grey Cup championship teams—Toronto (1991) and Edmonton (1993). He returned to the United States to play in the Arena Football League. His first Arena League experience was with the Minnesota Fighting Pike. Foggie passed for 2,269 yards and 40 touchdowns for the Pike, who went 4-10 and folded after the one season (1996) of playing at Target Center. Foggie went on to play eight more seasons in the Arena League.

Foggie, who works in the mortgage lending business, has started building his coaching resume as well. Foggie has spent three seasons as an assistant in the Arena Football 2 League, whose season runs from March to July. Foggie also expected to be the offensive coordinator for the Burnsville High School football team in 2007.

Chapter 16

CHIP LOHMILLER

EARLY LIFE OF CHIP LOHMILLER

Moving around isn't always a positive thing for a child. But for Chip Lohmiller, who lived in three states in a four-year span, it was a positive experience.

Each move exposed Lohmiller to a skill that would eventually carry him to the NFL.

"We lived in Woodbury (Minnesota) until I was in fifth grade," said Lohmiller. "Then my father, who worked for 3M, got transferred. When we left he always said we'd be back (in Woodbury) in three years."

The Lohmillers first stop was Chatham, New Jersey.

"One of my coaches in fifth grade started me kicking," said Lohmiller.

From New Jersey, the Lohmillers moved to Dallas.

"I was in the seventh grade, in middle school," said Lohmiller. "I got there in the middle of the football season and the kicker was already established. His name was Chris Jacke. I got to know him. He went on to kick in college (at Texas-El Paso) and in the NFL for 11 seasons (eight with the Green Bay Packers). It (moving) wasn't too bad; we got to see the country a little and then we moved back to Woodbury."

NAME: John Mcleod Lohmiller
BORN: July 16, 1966
POSITION: Kicker
HEIGHT: 6-3
WEIGHT: 213
YEARS: 1984-1987
ACCOMPLISHMENTS: First team
 All-Big Ten (1986).
GAME: vs. Michigan—November
 15, 1986

Once he got to Woodbury High School, Lohmiller was again exposed to someone who helped further his interest in kicking.

"I had a great coach in high school," said Lohmiller. "His name was Mark Porter. He really emphasized special teams. Most high school coaches treat special teams as an afterthought. But he really emphasized it."

In addition to kicking, Lohmiller also punted and played wide receiver and safety for the Royals.

"We were pretty good my junior and senior years," said Lohmiller. "We were 7-1, 7-2. Stillwater was in our conference and they were good every year. We finally beat them when I was a senior."

Lohmiller started getting attention from college football programs, including the University of Minnesota.

"Coach (Joe) Salem was recruiting me," said Lohmiller. "And I had offers from a couple of Division II programs."

Before Lohmiller made his decision, there was a coaching change at the University of Minnesota. Salem announced in October of 1983 that he would step down at the end of the season.

On December 22, 1983, Lou Holtz, who had resigned as the Arkansas coach four days earlier, was named the Gophers' coach.

"Coach Holtz came to our house," said Lohmiller. "He was quite a salesman. I knew I wanted to stay around home. I decided I wanted to play for the University and walked on."

As a freshman walk-on in 1984, Chip Lohmiller (25) beat out 13 other kickers for the starting job.

Lohmiller arrived on the University campus in the fall of 1984, with plenty of competition for a roster spot.

"When I came in as a freshman there were 14 kickers," said Lohmiller. "There were a couple of junior college transfers, a couple of walk-ons. Coach Holtz basically had a competition. It came down to me and Charlie Horton."

Lohmiller won the job.

Lohmiller had a successful freshman season—leading the Gophers in scoring with 53 points by kicking 11 field goals and converting 20 extra-point kicks. The Gophers, who had gone 1-10 the previous season, went 4-7 overall—highlighted by victories over Wisconsin and Iowa. The Gophers went 3-6 in the Big Ten after winning just one of their previous 20 Big Ten games.

SETTING

The Gophers improved quickly in their second season under Holtz.

They opened the 1985 season with five victories in their first six games. The only loss in that span was a 13-7 loss to No. 1-ranked Oklahoma.

Back-to-back losses to Ohio State (by four points) and Michigan (by five points) dropped the Gophers to 5-3. But the Gophers defeated Wisconsin, 27-18, to become bowl-eligible for the first time since 1977.

The Gophers lost their final two regular-season games to finish 6-5 before the program was stunned by the sudden departure of Holtz. Four days after the Gophers' 31-9 loss to Iowa in the regular-season finale, Holtz, who had three years remaining on his contract, accepted an offer to become the coach at Notre Dame.

"Coach Holtz did a lot for the program," said Lohmiller. "He got the practice facility built. We were selling out the Dome. He always talked to us about commitment to the program. We knew he had always wanted to coach at Notre Dame, so we respected that."

Gophers defensive coordinator John Gutekunst was the Gophers' interim coach.

"Gutey was a players' coach," said Lohmiller. "We respected him. He knew us. We didn't want change. We wanted him to get the job."

Gutekunst made his debut as the Gophers' head coach less than a month later in the Gophers' 21-13 victory over Clemson in the Independence Bowl in Shreveport, Louisiana.

The victory gave the Gophers their most successful season (seven victories) since 1977.

The Gophers opened the 1986 season with a 31-7 victory over Bowling Green, but the following week were trampled by the Oklahoma Sooners, 63-0.

"I remember they had a tight end named Keith Jackson," said Lohmiller. "He had one touchdown of 95 yards. We couldn't catch him. He was that good."

The following week the Gophers were stunned by Pacific, 24-20, at home to fall to 1-2. But the Gophers regrouped with three consecutive victories—Purdue (36-9), Northwestern (44-23), and Indiana (19-17). Lohmiller's 21-yard field goal in the final five seconds was the winning margin against Indiana.

The Gophers suffered two more setbacks—to Ohio State (33-0) and to Michigan State (52-23). The loss to Ohio State was the first time the Gophers had been shut out in four seasons.

The Gophers rebounded with a 27-20 victory at Wisconsin to improve to 5-4 going into the showdown for the Little Brown Jug in Ann Arbor, Michigan.

Michigan brought a 13-game winning streak and 15-game unbeaten streak—both the longest active streaks in Division I-A football—into the game. Going into the game, the Wolverines also harbored realistic hopes of a Big Ten championship and a national championship.

Also looming for the Wolverines, who were installed as 25½ point favorites over the Gophers, was a showdown the next week with Ohio State, which was also unbeaten in the Big Ten.

The Wolverines, who also had a 14-game home winning streak, had beaten the Gophers eight consecutive times—including a 48-7 victory the previous year. In the eight previous meetings, the

Wolverines had outscored the Gophers, 333-96. The Wolverines had scored at least 48 points against the Gophers in three of the previous four years. The closest game in the streak as the Wolverines' 31-21 victory in 1979.

GAME OF MY LIFE

BY CHIP LOHMILLER

Going into the Michigan game, I think things were going all right for us. There were some positive things happening in the program.

Going into a game at Michigan, you think how big the stadium was and how good they were.

But we had some talent and a pretty powerful offense.

Of all our team rivalries, Michigan and the Little Brown Jug was the biggest.

(Assistant) coach (Butch) Nash would talk about the rivalries and the significance of the item (trophy) for each game. He talked to us the night before the game. He talked to us about the 1977 game, when the Gophers upset Michigan.

He was a great speaker and he was passionate about Gopher football. For guys on the team who weren't too familiar with the rivalries, he embedded into their soul what it meant to the team, the school, the community, and the state. He showed us what it meant. It was a great speech.

One thing I really remember from the game is Rickey (Foggie) scrambling around and making yards on the last drive.

Rickey, Darrell Thompson, and I did a lot together (off the field). It does ring a bell that we talked later how there was talk at the end of the game about just sitting on it and playing for the tie.

When I was on the sideline getting ready for a kick, I was focused on putting positive images in my mind: where the ball was going to be on the field and what type of kick it was going to be. I always focused on positive thoughts. What you have to do in that situation is visualize that you're putting it down the middle. That's what Coach Holtz always stressed to all of us: positive imagery. That carried with me into the NFL. I stressed it throughout my career.

Before the kick, the crowd had been going nuts. After I made the kick, suddenly there was silence. Our band, down in one corner of the stadium, was the only noise. That's my biggest memory.

GAME RESULTS

Lohmiller's 30-yard field goal as time ran out silenced the Michigan Stadium crowd of 104,864 and lifted the Gophers to a 20-17 victory.

During a timeout with less than a minute to go, junior quarterback Rickey Foggie and coach John Gutekunst, the third coach Gophers seniors had played under during their Gophers careers, considered their options.

They discussed taking the conservative approach, running out the clock and taking the tie. But Foggie had a different idea.

"We're not even supposed to be in the game. Basically we said, 'What the heck? Let's just go for it,'" Foggie recalled for the *Minneapolis Star Tribune* in 2003. "I knew once we got inside the 40, Ol' Chip could put it through. He's got a great leg."

With 47 seconds remaining, Foggie scrambled for 31 yards after being unable to find an open receiver to give the Gophers the ball at the Michigan 17-yard line. After Thompson's three-yard run, the ball was spotted in the middle of the field at the 14-yard line.

Lohmiller calmly kicked the field goal. "It was right down the middle," Lohmiller told the *Minneapolis Star Tribune* in 2003. "I knew I had it."

The Gophers scored first—on a 15-yard pass from Foggie to Mel Anderson—before the Wolverines kicked a field goal to make it 7-3. On the ensuing kickoff, the Wolverines got a break when the ball hit at the Gophers' 11-yard line and then bounced backwards almost 20 yards, where the Wolverines recovered. Four plays later, the Wolverines scored to take a 10-7 lead.

The Gophers scored 10 points in the third quarter to take a 17-14 lead. A 25-yard field goal by Lohmiller put the Gophers in the lead. It was the first time all season the Wolverines had been outscored in the third quarter.

The Gophers, who forced four Michigan turnovers, got the ball back with 2:20 remaining.

Leading up to game, Michigan coach Bo Schembechler told newspapers, "It would be a disaster for us if we lost this game."

The first loss of the season dropped the Wolverines to No. 6 in the Top 25 poll. The following week, the Wolverines bounced back to defeat No. 7 Ohio State, 26-24, to earn a trip to the Rose Bowl, where they lost to Arizona State, 22-15.

The stunning victory over the Wolverines improved the Gophers to 6-4—making them bowl eligible for a second consecutive season. The following week, the Gophers closed out the regular season with a 30-27 loss to the Iowa Hawkeyes, despite a school-record 62-yard field goal by Lohmiller.

The Gophers accepted a bid to play Tennessee in the Liberty Bowl—just the second time in school history that the Gophers had played in a bowl game in back-to-back seasons. The only other time was the 1961 and 1962 Rose Bowls.

Tennessee defeated the Gophers, 21-14.

WHAT HAPPENED TO CHIP LOHMILLER?

In 1987, Lohmiller's senior season, the Gophers opened with five consecutive victories—their best start to a season since the national championship season in 1960.

But in week six, the Gophers suffered their first loss—a one-point loss to Indiana—when Lohmiller missed a 44-yard field goal with 1:30 remaining. The Gophers lost their next three games to drop to 5-4. A 22-19 victory over Wisconsin ended the losing streak, but the season ended with a 34-20 loss at Iowa. Despite a 6-5 record, the Gophers didn't get a bowl invitation.

For his Gophers career, Lohmiller converted 95 of 97 extra-point kicks and 57 of 75 field goals (78 percent). At the time, he was the leading scorer in school history (268 points). In 2002, Dan Nystrom became the leader with 367 points.

In April of 1988, the Super Bowl champion Washington Redskins selected Lohmiller in the second round (the Redskins didn't have a pick in the first round) of the NFL draft. Lohmiller would go on to play nine seasons in the NFL.

In 1991, his fourth season in the league, Lohmiller led the NFL in scoring with 149 points, and following the season, the Redskins advanced to Super Bowl XXVI, which was played at the Metrodome in Minneapolis. The Redskins defeated the Buffalo Bills, 37-24. Kicking on familiar turf, Lohmiller booted three field goals and converted four extra points.

Lohmiller spent seven seasons with the Redskins before finishing his career with New Orleans (in 1995) and St. Louis (1996). Lohmiller finished his career with 913 points, which ranks 47th on the NFL's all-time kickers scoring list.

Following his career, Lohmiller settled in Crosslake, Minnesota—20 miles north of Brainerd. Lohmiller runs a property management company and a construction business and is a volunteer fireman. In 2004, Lohmiller added another job—head football coach at Pequot Lakes High School.

"The opportunity was there," said Lohmiller. "The coach was leaving. I knew the kids, I had been an assistant coach since 2001, and enjoyed the coaching. I wanted to stay involved."

Chapter 17

DARRELL THOMPSON

EARLY LIFE OF DARRELL THOMPSON

Darrell Thompson doesn't remember a time from his childhood when he wasn't surrounded by sports.

"I've been in gyms since being born," said Thompson. "Both my mom and dad were very athletic. My mom played volleyball, basketball and softball. My dad played softball, flag football, and basketball. We were always in a gym.

"As I got older I started playing basketball with my dad, and it just evolved into me playing sports competitively—football, basketball, and track."

Thompson's father was an industrial engineer.

"My dad was recruited by IBM (in Thompson's hometown of Rochester, Minnesota)," said Thompson.

Thompson said his childhood in Rochester was pretty typical as he developed into a three-sport athlete at Rochester John Marshall High School.

By his senior year in high school, college football coaches had taken notice of the durable running back with speed (4.5 in the 40). As a senior, Thompson rushed for 1,370 yards (137 yards per game and 9.8 yards per carry) and 16 touchdowns. Following the season

NAME: Darrell Alexander
  Thompson
BORN: November 23, 1967
POSITION: Running back
HEIGHT: 6-2
WEIGHT: 205
YEARS: 1986-1989
ACCOMPLISHMENTS: All-Big Ten
  (1986); two-time team MVP.
GAME: vs. Bowling Green—
  September 13, 1986

he was named to the All-State football team.

"The recruiting experience was chaotic and fun," said Thompson. "it was a whirlwind."

Thompson made visits to Iowa, Nebraska, and Wisconsin. UCLA also recruited him.

"I was offered a visit by UCLA," said Thompson. "But I would have had to miss basketball practice, and my coach didn't want me to miss practice. So I didn't go."

Thompson said he had no preconceived notions about any of the schools.

"My mom was from Mississippi and my dad was from St. Louis," said Thompson, "so I didn't have any ties to Minnesota. I never went to Gopher games. I went to one or two Gopher basketball games.

"Every school I visited was great. All those places were exciting and new. Iowa City was cool. Wisconsin was great. At Iowa, Hayden Fry had some good teams during that time. I thought Iowa might be the place for me. My sister went to Iowa. My wife went there and played volleyball there. But it came down to where did I want to be if football didn't work out. I ended up picking Minnesota because of the business community, and they were good people who cared about what happened to you."

Thompson announced his decision in February of 1986 after scoring 14 points in Rochester John Marshall's 66-51 victory over rival Rochester Mayo.

Most observers considered Thompson the top player in the state and the top catch of 10 in-state recruits signed by the Gopher

Darrell Thompson's 98-yard run against Michigan in his sophomore season is the longest run ever against the Wolverines.

coaching staff. Thompson's commitment meant the Gophers had all the state players it sought for the first time in years.

"He was the guy we had to have," said Gophers coach John Gutekunst.

SETTING

Thompson's freshman season was also Gutekunst's first season as a head coach. Gutekunst, the Gophers' defensive coordinator the previous two seasons, had taken over as head coach in December of 1985 after Lou Holtz resigned to become the coach at Notre Dame.

Holtz had taken over two years earlier. In his first season (1984), Holtz led the Gophers to a 4-7 overall record and a 3-6 record in the Big Ten. The 3-6 conference record was an improvement over the previous two seasons, which saw the Gophers go 1-17 in the Big Ten. The Gophers' 33-24 victory over Indiana on October 1984 ended a 21-game losing streak in the Big Ten.

The Gophers opened Holtz's second season with five victories in their first six games. Their only loss in that stretch was a 13-7 loss to No. 3 Oklahoma before 62,446 at the Metrodome. A 22-7 victory over Indiana improved the Gophers to 5-1 and helped the Gophers earn a spot (No. 20) in the Associated Press Top 25 for the first time in three years. But the Gophers suffered back-to-back losses (by four points to No. 9 Ohio State and by five points to Michigan State) to fall to 5-3. A 27-18 victory over Wisconsin before 64,571 at the Metrodome made the Gophers bowl eligible. The Gophers closed the regular season with losses to No. 8 Michigan and No. 3 Iowa. Four days after the Iowa loss (November 27), Holtz resigned.

Gutekunst made his debut as the Gophers head coach when he directed the Gophers to a 20-13 victory over Clemson in the Independence Bowl on December 21, 1985.

Going into spring practice in 1986, the Gophers had 17 returning starters—seven on offense. During spring practice, no running back emerged as the clear-cut No. 1. During one scrimmage, 11 players carried the ball with the leading rusher gaining just 33 yards. Ed Penn, who was considered the No. 1 back, gained just 22 yards.

When practice opened in August of 1986, Gutekunst was still looking for a No. 1 tailback and a No. 1 fullback. The coach suggested the two positions were open to freshmen like Thompson, Ron Goetz, and Pat Tingelhoff.

Gutekunst told the *Minneapolis Star Tribune*, "I'm anxious to see the young freshmen. Not that I expect a great deal from them, but there is a place for several of them."

One week before the regular-season opener, the Gophers had another scrimmage. Penn, a sophomore from Tampa, Florida, scored a touchdown and gained 67 yards in six carries while Thompson gained 57 yards in five carries. Gutekunst said he was encouraged by the play of all of his running backs in the scrimmage but added that Penn had risen to the competition of the younger backs.

"Going into camp, I had no idea what to expect," Thompson said. "It was a little intimidating. I had no Division I experience. My goal was to survive every practice."

The Gophers opened the 1986 season at the Metrodome against Bowling Green of the Mid-America Conference. Both Gutekunst and Thompson would make their regular-season debuts for the Gophers.

GAME OF MY LIFE

BY DARRELL THOMPSON

The year before I was playing high school football against teams like Mankato East, Mankato West, Rochester Mayo, Winona, and Apple Valley.

This (college football) was a whole different beast. Practice was so different. Every five minutes was scripted. It was so organized. You had a position coach looking over your shoulder to make sure you were doing things right.

During his Gophers career, Darrell Thompson rushed for a school-record 4,654 yards and rushed for at least 100 yards 23 times.

I was nervous going into the (Bowling Green) game. It was a different team and there were over 50,000 fans in the stands. We drew a lot of people because of Lou Holtz.

I was really scared, kinda scared of everything. I guess I thought everything would be bigger, faster than anything I'd played in, but once it started it didn't seem that way. I just tried to make things go.

I just relaxed and told myself to "do what you do." I felt very comfortable.

I got my feet wet in the first half (gaining 27 yards in five carries) but we only had a 3-0 lead (on a 47-yard field goal by Chip Lohmiller) at halftime because we had fumbled three times (including once at the 4-yard line).

We got a boost right away at the start of the second half when Mel Anderson returned the second-half kickoff 46 yards to give us great field position. We started to move the ball, and I scored my first touchdown on a 10-yard run (to make it 9-0).

Two minutes later we got the ball back and I broke a 46-yard run and then scored on the next play on a 12-yard run. I scored two more touchdowns—one on a 60-yard run in the fourth quarter. I was still fresh because I had played only half the game.

The offensive line (which included center Ray Hitchcock, left tackle Norries Wilson, and left guard Paul Anderson) was outstanding. I was spoiled. I never had another offensive line like that one. And our quarterback, (junior) Ricky Foggie was really talented (Foggie had passed for 2,406 yards and rushed for 1,098 yards in his first two seasons.)

In the second half, the offensive line was really cranked up. I can't put it into words. They were blowing them off the offensive line. And I remember on that long run I had for a touchdown ... a wide receiver either Mel Anderson or Gary Couch making a block way down field to help. Those aren't easy blocks to make.

I was just a snotty-nosed kid. It was a big game for me, for selfish reasons, because it showed I could play.

When it was over, the Gophers' 31-7 victory over Bowling Green showed Thompson could play at the Division I level.

"(But) one game does not mean everything. It means something, but it still doesn't prove a lot," Thompson told the *Minneapolis Star Tribune*. "Am I making sense? What I mean is, I'm happy, but I still have to feel my way through things before I'm comfortable."

The freshman finished with 205 yards in 19 carries and tied a school single-game record with four touchdowns. The 205 yards were the most by a Gopher since Garry White had gained 230 against Wisconsin in 1979, and were the most yards for a Division I-A back playing in his first game, according to the NCAA (single-game records have existed since 1943).

Gutekunst said Thompson was "a great talent. We expect him to do nothing but get better. We know not all games will be like this one, but we think he will help us win football games. He's very mature. When he came into camp, he kept his mouth shut and he worked."

Gutekunst was asked if Thompson's running style reminded him of anyone. He responded, "It reminds me of Darrell Thompson."

The Gophers lost their next two games (at No. 1 Oklahoma, 63-0, and at home to Pacific). The Gophers then reeled off three consecutive victories to improve to 4-2. The final victory in that stretch was a 19-17 victory over Indiana, which saw Thompson rush for 191 yards.

Two losses dropped the Gophers to 4-4, but victories over Wisconsin (27-20) and No. 2 Michigan (20-17) made the Gophers bowl eligible. The Gophers lost their regular-season finale to Iowa (30-27) but were invited to play Tennessee in the Liberty Bowl in Memphis, Tennessee.

The bowl invitation meant the Gophers would make back-to-back trips to a bowl game for the first time in 25 years.

The Volunteers won the game, 21-14. Thompson rushed for 136 yards in the game—his seventh 100-yard rushing game of the season—which pushed his season total to 1,376 yards.

Thompson's sophomore season was highlighted by a 98-yard touchdown run against Michigan—the longest run ever against the Wolverines, who won the game at the Metrodome, 30-20. Thompson finished the 6-5 season with 1,229 yards and 13 touchdowns.

The Gophers were 2-7-2 in Thompson's junior season as he fell 90 yards short of his third consecutive 1,000-yard season.

As a senior, Thompson rushed for 1,139 yards to finish his career with a school-record 4,654 yards. During his career, he rushed for 100 yards in a game 23 times and rushed for 40 touchdowns.

Despite going 6-5 in 1987 and 1989, the Gophers were not invited to a bowl game. The Gophers were 4-4 (tied for fifth place) in the Big Ten in 1989.

WHAT HAPPENED TO DARRELL THOMPSON?

In April of 1990, Thompson was selected in the first round (the 19th player selected overall) of the NFL draft by the Green Bay Packers.

Thompson went on to play five seasons for the Packers. His best season was 1993 when he rushed for 654 yards. He retired after being cut by the Chicago Bears in 1995.

"The NFL was a great experience," said Thompson. "I tried to continue what I did in college—keep my mouth shut and play hard."

During the off-seasons, Thompson began volunteering.

"I started for the Minneapolis Jaycees," said Thompson. "The guy who got me started was Ira Smith, the grandfather of current Gophers basketball player Brandon Smith. Then I started working for them part-time—speaking to kids. The Jaycees wanted to do something more for kids, and Bolder Options was created under the Jaycees umbrella."

Since 1995, Thompson has been the executive director of Bolder Options, a nonprofit youth mentoring program. According to Bolder Options' web site, the program focuses its efforts on at-risk kids 10-14 years old, and offers mentor-youth interaction through running and biking.

"When we started, our budget was $30,000 and we had six kids in a three-month program. The next year we had 11 kids and I thought it was great because we had almost doubled in one year. This year (2006) we have 106 kids in a year-long program, and our budget is $1.5 million.

"The program has been a success, but not just because of me. At the start, I was able to open a few doors. But the success of the program doesn't hinge on me. It's successful because the program works."

Chapter 18

TYRONE CARTER

EARLY LIFE OF TYRONE CARTER

When Tyrone Carter was seven years old, he and his older brother Tony went to live with their grandmother, Mamie.

"She's a church-going woman," Carter told the *Minneapolis Star Tribune*. "She made us go to church every Sunday. She taught us the values of life, told us who to hang around."

Tony Carter, a good high school football player, didn't heed his grandmother's advice. He dropped out of school and moved away. His grandmother wouldn't let Tyrone repeat his brother's choices.

"She made sure I had something to do in church every week and she made me play sports all year-round," Tyrone Carter told the *Minneapolis Star Tribune*. "And if I didn't do well in school, I had to go to church every time she went and I couldn't play sports."

Carter, who also benefited from the influence of 18 uncles (one who taught him how to box at the age of 11), became an outstanding offensive and defensive player for Ely High School in Pompano Beach, Florida.

Carter earned first team offensive and defensive All-County honors. As a senior, he rushed for 1,349 yards and scored 23 touchdowns. His touchdown total included kickoff returns of 90, 95, and 97 yards for touchdowns. His abilities caught the attention of many schools, including Gophers assistant coach Kevin Sumlin.

NAME: Tyrone Carter
BORN: March 31, 1976
POSITION: Safety
HEIGHT: 5-8
WEIGHT: 190
YEARS: 1996-1999
ACCOMPLISHMENTS: First team
    All-Big Ten (1998, 1999);
    first team All-America (1998,
    1999); Jim Thorpe Award
    winner (1999).
GAME: vs. Penn State—
    November 6, 1999

But Carter, who had a 3.0 GPA in high school, didn't qualify academically for a scholarship for the 1995 season, because his ACT test score wasn't high enough. The Gophers promised to hold a scholarship if he passed the test. After he passed the test in October of 1995, he chose Minnesota over Pittsburgh, Mississippi, and Michigan State and enrolled in January of 1996 and took part in spring practice.

Carter's first season with the Gophers was a rollercoaster.

"My freshman year, I was up and down with my coaches," said Carter. "But I have to take my hat off to Jim Wacker. He gave me a chance to play.

"That first year was my lowest low. I told my grandmother that I might transfer. She convinced me to stay. She'd said, 'Things happen all the time in life. You just have to overcome them and change it around.' I bought into that."

The season did provide one highlight for Carter and the Gophers. Gophers opened the 1996 season—Wacker's fifth as the Gophers coach—with victories over Northeast Louisiana (30-3) and Ball State (26-23). The third game on the Gophers' 1996 schedule presented a bigger challenge—No. 23 Syracuse, which was led by quarterback Donovan McNabb—and provided Carter with his first start for the Gophers.

Always wanting to make an impact on the field, Tyrone Carter continues to do so as a defensive back in the NFL.

SETTING

Carter immediately made his presence known. Carter set an NCAA record when he returned two fumbles for touchdowns in a 56-second span in the third quarter to help the Gophers outlast the Orangemen, 35-33, before nearly 46,000 at the Metrodome. Carter's first touchdown was a 63-yard return, which gave the Gophers a 15-12 lead. Less than a minute later, he returned a fumble 20 yards for a touchdown to make it 22-12.

"I had always wanted to make my presence known on the field," said Carter, "and to get the opportunity against a team like Syracuse and Donovan McNabb was great. I just wanted to be the best safety on the field. Everything happened so fast. I was fortunate to return two fumbles for touchdowns, make a couple of hits and some good plays."

The victory over the Orangemen gave the Gophers a 3-0 start for the first time in five seasons, but the next week the Gophers suffered a three-point loss to Purdue—the first of six consecutive losses. The following week, the Gophers suffered a tough two-point loss to No. 15 Northwestern. The Gophers won just one of their final eight games to finish with a 4-7 record—1-7 in the Big Ten.

Wacker resigned following the season, and about three weeks later, Kansas coach Glen Mason was hired.

The Gophers opened the 1997 season by winning two of their first three games under Mason, but then suffered a seven-game losing streak. That streak was fueled by three losses to teams ranked in the top ten in a four-week span.

The Gophers showed improvement in Mason's second season—Carter's junior season. The Gophers were 4-3 before three consecutive losses left them with a 4-6 record heading into the season-finale against Iowa. An impressive 49-7 victory over the Hawkeyes was the Gophers' second conference victory—the first time in five seasons the Gophers had won more than one conference game in a season—and left them with a 5-6 record. Following the season Carter was named first team All-Big Ten and first team All-

America. Carter had recorded 158 tackles and eight sacks in 11 games.

The Gophers opened the 1999 season with four consecutive victories (Ohio University, Louisiana-Monroe, Illinois State, and Northwestern) for their first 4-0 start to a season since 1987.

But the Gophers lost to three ranked opponents in their next four games to fall to 5-3. The three losses were by a total of 11 points—three-point losses to No. 20 Wisconsin (in overtime) and No. 22 Ohio State, and a four-point loss to No. 18 Purdue.

Next on the schedule for the Gophers was a trip to Pennsylvania and a game against No. 2 Penn State. The odds didn't favor the Gophers. The unbeaten Nittany Lions (9-0), who had won the previous four games between the two teams, were 14-point favorites, while the Gophers, who hadn't beaten a top-five-ranked team since 1986, were just 4-29 in Big Ten Conference road games since 1991.

GAME OF MY LIFE

BY TYRONE CARTER

Two years earlier (when Penn State was ranked No. 1 and favored by 34 points over the Gophers) we played them close but lost to them by one point after we lost a fumble. We should have beaten them. But the (16-15) loss told us we could play with them.

The year before (Penn State was No. 13) we played them tough at home but got beat by 10 points.

We went into this game with them ranked No. 1 or No. 2, looking at ourselves as a program on the rise. It definitely was a challenge for us. For myself, there is no doubt it was a big challenge. As an athlete you want to challenge yourself. You want to play the top schools and the top athletes. You want to play Michigan, Ohio State, and Penn State.

I always feel I have to measure myself out there every game, and I hate to lose.

(That day) I was just flying around out there trying to make things happen. I think I had 20 tackles that game. I was trying to be all over the field.

In the second half it was just back and forth. (The Nittany Lions scored on three consecutive possession) but we were finally able to get a stop and get the ball back.

(Before the final scoring play) there were 96,000 fans going crazy. I remember thinking on the sideline that we had the opportunity to win and I didn't want anything to happen to our freshman kicker (Dan Nystrom).

I just didn't want to watch (when he lined up for a field-goal attempt). I thanked the Lord for giving us another opportunity. Then I put my head down and said a prayer. I knew it was good when players started jumping up and down and one of them hit me. Then I thanked the Lord again. The crowd was so quiet, you could hear a pin drop. All we did was run off the field.

There is no doubt we felt like we were writing history. We had beaten a powerhouse like Penn State, and I felt that we were just a small-school program. I think the victory gave us exposure nationally (the game was televised nationally on ESPN2) and it helped get us more recruits.

It showed that a hard week of practice paid off, and it put us in the spotlight. It gave us a lot of confidence.

GAME RESULTS

Penn State had scored late in the first half to take a 14-9 lead at halftime. Early in the third quarter, the Nittany Lions added to their lead with a field goal.

Late in the third quarter, the Gophers pulled within two, 17-15, on a three-yard touchdown run by quarterback Billy Cockerham. A two-point conversion attempt failed.

After his last game with the Gophers, Tyrone Carter was the NCAA all-time leader in solo tackles (414) and tackles (528) by a defensive back.

The Nittany Lions settled for another three points—a 44-yard field goal by Travis Forney—to take a 20-15 lead.

But running back Thomas Hamner, who had committed the crucial fumble in the loss to Penn State two years earlier, caught a 49-yard touchdown pass from Cockerham to give the Gophers a 21-20 lead. Another failed two-point conversion kept the Gophers' lead at one point.

Penn State responded with its third consecutive scoring drive as Forney kicked another 44-yard field goal to put the Nittany Lions up 23-21. The Nittany Lions then stopped the Gophers on the ensuing possession to get the ball back, but the Gophers defense rose to the occasion and forced Penn State to punt.

The Gophers took possession at their own 20-yard line with 1:50 remaining. On the first play, Cockerham completed a 46-yard pass to Ron Johnson to give the Gophers the ball at the Penn State 34-yard line. Three plays—two incompletions and a six-yard sack—left the Gophers with a 4th-and-6 at the Penn State 40.

Cockerham threw another pass in Johnson's direction, but the pass bounced off Johnson and appeared to be an incompletion. But the Gophers' Arland Bruce dove and caught the deflection to give the Gophers a first down at the Nittany Lions' 13.

Three plays later—and after a timeout with two seconds remaining—Nystrom, an 18-year old freshman—kicked a 32-yard field goal as time ran out to give the Gophers a 24-23 victory, which made the Gophers bowl eligible for the first time since 1986. The victory also gave the Gophers a 4-0 record in conference road games for the first time since 1961.

The Gophers closed out the season with victories over Indiana and Iowa to finish 8-3—their first eight-victory season since 1961. The Gophers closed out the season with a 24-20 loss to Oregon in the Sun Bowl in El Paso, Texas.

In the Sun Bowl, Carter had 18 tackles—eight solo—to become the NCAA all-time leader in solo tackles (414) and tackles (528) by a Division I-A defensive back. Carter, who was a repeat first team

All-Big Ten and All-America selection, won the Jim Thorpe Award as the top defensive back in the nation. Carter, the first Gopher to be named All-America in consecutive seasons since Bob Stein in 1967 and 1968, was selected over finalists Deon Grant of Tennessee and Brian Urlacher of New Mexico.

The durable Carter did not miss a practice or game (playing in 45 games with 43 consecutive starts) during his Gophers career.

"Tyrone is the most complete defensive back I've been around," Gophers defensive coordinator David Gibbs told the *Minneapolis Star Tribune*. "He can cover like a corner and he tackles like a linebacker."

WHAT HAPPENED TO TYRONE CARTER?

Following his senior season, Carter was selected by the Minnesota Vikings in the fourth round (118th player overall) of the 2000 NFL draft.

In his rookie season, he started seven regular-season games and also started in the NFC championship game against the New York Giants.

He spent two more seasons with the Vikings before spending the 2003 season with the New York Jets. In that season, he had a career-high 53 solo tackles and 88 tackles.

Carter re-signed with the Vikings in 2004 but was released by the Vikings right before the regular-season opener. On October 20 he signed with the Pittsburgh Steelers. He spent the rest of the season with the Steelers, playing mostly on special teams. The Steelers reached the AFC Championship game following the season.

In 2005, Carter was backup safety and special teams member while appearing in all 16 regular-season games for the Steelers. Carter also played in each of the Steelers' four postseason games. Carter had three tackles (two solo) in the Steelers' 21-10 victory over the Seattle Seahawks in Super Bowl XL.

"After the adversity I had gone through, playing in a Super Bowl was so rewarding," said Carter. "To make it to the NFL and then to get to play in the Super Bowl is special."

Carter returned to the Steelers in 2006 and appeared in all 16 regular-season games. After starting the season with just two victories in their first eight games, the Steelers went 6-2 in their final eight games but just missed the playoffs.

"I don't take anything for granted," said Carter, following his seventh NFL season. "I'm so grateful I was fortunate enough to play in the NFL. I'll never get complacent. I have to prove myself each year."

Chapter 19

MATT SPAETH

EARLY LIFE OF MATT SPAETH

Even though Ken Spaeth had played football at Nebraska and was drafted by the Buffalo Bills of the NFL, he didn't push his sons to play football.

"He never forced us," said Matt Spaeth. "He was supportive and encouraged us. But my brother and I were already really into sports when he started encouraging us."

Matt Spaeth's first love was basketball.

"Growing up," said Spaeth, "I wanted to play basketball in college. I played on an AAU select team that traveled all over the country. The only time I wasn't playing basketball was during football season."

Spaeth developed into an outstanding basketball and football player at St. Michael-Albertville High School. In his sophomore season, the Knights reached the State Class 3A Championship Game. Spaeth was named the defensive MVP of the game, which was won by De La Salle, 28-7. The Knights reached the section final the next year and the section semifinals in Spaeth's senior season.

"De La Salle was a pretty good team," said Spaeth. "I thought we had our best team the next year. As a senior we moved up to (Class) 4A and nobody expected much out of us, but it turned out we had a good season. We went 12-1. Our only loss was in the

189

NAME: Matthew John Spaeth
BORN: November 24, 1983
POSITION: Tight end
HEIGHT: 6-7
WEIGHT: 265
YEARS: 2003-2006
ACCOMPLISHMENTS: First team
   All-Big Ten (2005, 2006); first
   team All-America (2006); John
   Mackey Award winner (2006).
GAME: vs. Michigan—October 8,
   2005

section semifinals to (eventual state champion) Detroit Lakes. But we were without our running back, who was sixth in the state in rushing, and our quarterback was playing on what we thought was a sprained ankle. It turned out it was broken."

As a two-way starter as a senior, Spaeth caught 22 passes for 294 yards and three touchdowns, while on defense he had 203 tackles and eight interceptions.

In basketball Spaeth was a three-year letterman and three-time all-conference player. As a junior, Spaeth started getting recruited by some major Division I football programs, and he was also being recruited by smaller Division I basketball programs.

"I was 6-7. I was big, but not that big for Division I basketball," said Spaeth. "I knew whatever sport I played in college I'd have to put forth the time and effort. I started realizing football was my future in college."

Spaeth eventually narrowed down his college options to the University of Minnesota, Wisconsin, and his father's alma mater—Nebraska.

"They're all good schools and good programs," said Spaeth. "But it came down to Minnesota. I didn't think I was going to like the campus, but after my visit, I realized I really liked it. And I decided I wanted to stay close to home."

Matt Spaeth made 109 receptions in his Gophers career—the most in school history by a tight end.

Spaeth joined the Gophers program in the fall and was red-shirted as the Gophers went 7-5 in the regular season before beating Arkansas in the Music City Bowl.

Spaeth began his career as a defensive end. The transition from high school to college football wasn't smooth.

"To be quite honest with you," Gophers coach Glen Mason told the *Minneapolis Star Tribune* in August of 2006, "we thought maybe we had him overrated as a player, so we figured we would move him to tight end as a temporary stop and try and build him up to offensive tackle. As soon was we moved him over there, he seemed like a natural."

SETTING

As a red-shirt freshman in 2003, Spaeth appeared in 13 games and moved into the starting lineup for good with five games remaining in the season. On the season, he caught 12 passes for 98 yards and was named to *The Sporting News* Big Ten All-Freshman team and to the Rivals.com Freshman All-America team.

As a sophomore, Spaeth started all 12 games and was third on the team with 24 receptions despite playing the entire season with a sports hernia, which required surgery following the season.

Both the 2003 and 2004 seasons for the Gophers were defined by a tough loss to Michigan.

In 2003, the Gophers had opened with three nonconference victories to break into the Associated Press Top 25 poll at No. 24. Three more victories (Louisiana-Lafayette, Penn State, and Northwestern) improved the Gophers to 6-0 and moved them up seven spots to No. 17 in the poll. It was the first time since 1960 that the Gophers had opened a season 6-0.

Next up was Michigan, which was ranked No. 20. The pregame talk centered on the 100th anniversary of the first Little Brown Jug game and on the game being moved to Friday night to accommodate the Minnesota Twins playoff game at the Metrodome. A crowd of 62,374 and a national television audience saw the Gophers take a 28-7 lead into the fourth quarter. But the Wolverines scored 31 points in the fourth quarter to rally for a stunning 38-35 victory over the Gophers, who had rushed for 427 yards and outgained the Wolverines, 495-483.

The Gophers slumped the next week—losing to Michigan State. They rebounded with victories over Illinois, Indiana, and Wisconsin before losing their regular-season finale to Iowa. The Gophers capped the season by defeating Oregon in the Sun Bowl for their 10th victory—their most victories in a season since 1905.

The Gophers began the 2004 season ranked No. 22 in the Associated Press preseason Top 25 and opened the season with five consecutive victories to move up to No. 13 heading into another showdown with the Wolverines. A Michigan Stadium crowd of 111,518 and a national television audience saw the Gophers and the No. 14 Wolverines go down to the wire again.

Michigan led 17-14 at halftime, but the Gophers took a 21-17 lead into the fourth quarter. A 27-yard field goal by Rhys Lloyd gave the Gophers a 24-17 lead with 13:14 remaining. The Wolverines kicked a field goal with 9:36 remaining to pull within four, but they still trailed 24-20 when they got the ball back with 3:04 remaining. Chad Henne quickly directed the Wolverines downfield—capping a six-play, 87-yard scoring drive with a 31-yard touchdown pass with 1:57 remaining—to rally the Wolverines to a 27-24 victory.

The Gophers lost four of their next five games to finish the regular season with a 6-5 record but rebounded to defeat Alabama in the Music City Bowl.

The Gophers opened the 2005 season with victories over Tulsa, Colorado State, and Florida Atlantic to take a 3-0 record into a game with No. 11 Purdue.

Purdue took a 28-20 lead with 5:45 remaining when a pass intended for Spaeth was intercepted and returned 29 yards for a touchdown. But the Gophers responded with a 65-yard drive—finished off by an eight-yard touchdown reception by Spaeth with 1:34 remaining to pull within, 28-26. The Gophers converted the two-point conversion to tie the game and force overtime. In overtime, Purdue scored first, but the Gophers again rallied for a 42-35 victory in two overtimes.

The victory broke a seven-game losing streak to the Boilermakers and was the Gophers' first over a ranked opponent in three years.

"That was such a big win," said Spaeth. "It was our Big Ten opener and it gave us confidence to win a showdown like that."

The euphoria came to an abrupt end the next week as the Gophers were trampled by Penn State, 44-14.

Up next was a game against the Wolverines in Michigan.

GAME OF MY LIFE

BY MATT SPAETH

Anytime you get beat like we did at Penn State, it's a wakeup call. When you come back to practice you don't hang your head, you just have a new attitude. We had been embarrassed, so we had a hard week of practice (leading up to the Michigan game). We really re-energized our efforts that week.

During the week, the previous two Michigan games were brought up. But the coaching staff didn't preach to us. They didn't need to.

Michigan took advantage of a fumble to score and take a 13-3 late in the first half. But we were able to get a touchdown right before halftime to pull within three. Momentum is so huge, especially going into halftime. We went into the locker room knowing we hadn't played our best, but we were still only down by three points.

We tied it up early in the third quarter, but Steve Breaston returned the (ensuing) kickoff 95 yards for a touchdown. But we came back and put together a long scoring drive to tie the score again. Putting together a long drive is the best accomplishment an offense can have, and it felt good.

In 2006, Matt Spaeth became the first Gophers tight end in 35 years to earn All-America honors.

(One) thing people forget is that the (scoreboard) clock wasn't working the final minutes of the game. We had the ball and the officials were telling us the time, but it was hard to keep track.

It was tied 20-20 in their house. We had our backup quarterback (Tony Mortensen) in the game, because our starter (Bryan Cupito) had gotten hurt. Tony had only played a little against Colorado State earlier in the season and not much else.

So when we got the ball back, we just ran the ball and said, "Let's see what happens." I don't think we wanted to do anything crazy. We were just playing for overtime.

We lined up for a third down deep in our territory. We had been running the inside/outside zone blocking about 70 percent of the game. Michigan lined up looking like a blitz and ran the play and it worked (a 61-yard run by Gary Russell). We kicked a field goal with one second remaining, so we still had to kick off. And that was scary, especially with a guy like Breaston back there. He had already returned one for a touchdown. The ball got pitched and latereled around and those plays are scary. (It) happens more than you would think, where they're able to spring a guy free. Fortunately, we stopped them.

It was an amazing day.

GAME RESULTS

Russell's run—on a 3rd-and-10 with 1:27 remaining gave the Gophers a first down at the Michigan 13-yard line and silenced the crowd of 111,117. Spaeth and receiver Jared Ellerson had outstanding blocks to spring the run.

Three players later, Jason Giannini kicked a 30-yard field goal for a 23-20 lead with one second remaining.

The Gophers defense, which had given up 364 rushing yards the previous week to Penn State, gave up only 94 yards in the victory over Michigan. The Gophers' ground game, which had been limited to 113 yards by Penn State, gained 264 yards. Laurence Maroney (129 yards) and Russell (128) combined for 257 yards.

"It's a special moment for us right now, especially for our seniors," coach Glen Mason told the *Minneapolis Star Tribune*. "They put a tremendous amount into this game. And it wasn't just last week or since last year. When we lost a couple of years ago when we were up by 21 points in the fourth quarter, it really hasn't sat well with a lot of my guys. They talked about it quite a bit, and it really kind of festered inside of them. I was kind of hoping we wouldn't go to overtime. But I was willing to do that. But at the same time, every once in a while you have a gut feeling."

The victory ended the Gophers' 16-game losing streak to the Wolverines and was their first over Michigan since 1986. It was just the Gophers' third victory over Michigan in the last 36 meetings.

The Gophers lost to Wisconsin and Ohio State in the next two weeks, but defeated Indiana to become bowl eligible and then defeated Michigan State before losing their regular-season finale to Iowa. The Gophers' season ended with a loss to Virginia in the Music City Bowl.

Spaeth finished the season with 26 receptions for 333 yards and four touchdowns to earn first team All-Big Ten honors.

Spaeth went into his senior season as one of the team's co-captains and was mentioned as a preseason All-American.

The 2006 season was a rollercoaster for Spaeth and the Gophers. The Gophers won two of their first three games, but then lost four consecutive games to fall to 2-5. A 10-9 victory over North Dakota State ended the losing streak but was costly as Spaeth suffered a shoulder separation, which would require surgery.

Spaeth, who had started 37 consecutive games, sat out the next game—a 44-0 loss to Ohio State—but surprised many people when he returned to the lineup against Indiana just two weeks after the injury.

"A lot of people told me I shouldn't play," said Spaeth. "The doctors thought I might be able to come back for the (regular-season finale) Iowa game. I tried it against Indiana. I didn't think I'd be able to last the whole game. During the practice before the game, I bumped into someone and it hurt. It really hurt. But I still wanted to try it. I didn't want to regret later that I hadn't tried."

WHAT HAPPENED TO MATT SPAETH?

With Spaeth in the lineup, the Gophers won their final three regular-season games (Indiana, Michigan State, and Iowa) to finish with a 6-6 record and earn a trip to their seventh bowl game in eight seasons.

Spaeth had five catches for 44 yards and a touchdown in the victory over Iowa, which ended a five-game losing streak to the Hawkeyes and made the Gophers bowl eligible.

"That was the most emotional game of my career," said Spaeth. "We beat Iowa and everyone was happy. I was happy for my teammates but sad because I knew it was my last game."

Spaeth, who had surgery following the Iowa game, was rewarded with first team All-Big Ten and first team All-America honors. Spaeth, the first Gophers tight end to be named All-America since Doug Kingsriter in 1971, also won the John Mackey award as the nation's top Division I-A tight end.

"Even if I hadn't won any awards," said Spaeth, "it was worth it to come back and play."

For the season, Spaeth had 47 receptions—a school single-season record for tight ends—for 564 yards and four touchdowns. His career totals of 109 receptions for 1,293 yards were school records for a tight end. The 109 receptions are the ninth-best career total in school history.

While the Gophers prepared for their bowl game, Spaeth went through rehab for his shoulder. The rehab was going to prevent Spaeth from being able to work out at the NFL draft combine in Febuary of 2007. Spaeth, considered one of the top five tight ends available for the NFL draft, was still expected to go to the combine for the interview process.

"It's been hard to be patient," said Spaeth in late January. "Other guys are able to work out to get ready for the combine. But my shoulder feels good and my doctor is pleased with its progress. I just have to be patient."

Spaeth's patience was rewarded when the Pittsburgh Steelers selected him in the third round of the 2007 NFL draft.

Chapter 20

BRYAN CUPITO

EARLY LIFE OF BRYAN CUPITO

Bryan Cupito said there is no doubt sports were an integral part of his adolescence.

"Definitely," said Cupito. "Sports was my upbringing. Every day we played sports. I played on all kinds of teams—basketball, baseball ,and football. When I wasn't on a team, I was in the front yard playing sports with my brother."

Cupito grew in Cincinnati, Ohio, in a sports-minded family.

Cupito's grandfather played professional baseball in the Chicago Cubs organization. His father played college football at Louisville and his older brother played football at Indiana University.

But the sports background didn't make Cupito feel pressured to play sports.

"My father let us do our own thing," Cupito said. "He got involved but he never pushed us. He never forced us to play any sport. We asked him for his advice all the time, but he never forced his opinion on us."

Cupito developed into a standout at McNicholas High School in Cincinnati. He was a three-year starter at quarterback and safety for McNicholas. He broke many of the school's passing records and set a state record with 92 career touchdown passes.

NAME: Bryan Cupito
BORN: June 29, 1984
POSITION: Quarterback
HEIGHT: 6-3
WEIGHT: 205
YEARS: 2003-2006
ACCOMPLISHMENTS: All-time
    school leader in passing yards.
GAME: vs. Iowa—November 18,
    2006

As a senior, he passed for 3,850 yards and 45 touchdowns. Following his senior year, he played well in the Ohio North/South All-Star Football Game in Columbus. Cupito passed for 101 yards and threw touchdown passes of 34 and 48 yards.

"I wasn't that big of a recruit," said Cupito. "I probably had about 10 scholarship offers. My final five choices were Minnesota, Louisville, Marshall, Cincinnati, and Miami of Ohio. I made a couple of visits. I visited Minnesota and I really liked the campus and the city. That was one thing I was looking for—more than just a college campus. And I thought there was a great chance I'd get to play early."

Despite the gaudy statistics, Ohio State didn't recruit Cupito.

"They recruited another (Ohio) quarterback (Justin Zwick) the same year," said Cupito. "They told me right away. They were very up front about it."

Cupito arrived on the Minnesota campus in the fall of 2002 and redshirted. In 2003, as a redshirt freshman, he attempted just one pass as a backup to three-year starter Asad Abdul-Khaliq.

Cupito became the starter in 2004. On the season he completed 47 percent of his passes for 2,097 yards and threw 14 touchdown passes. He was intercepted just seven times in 261 attempts as the Gophers finished with a 6-5 regular-season record after starting the season 5-0. The Gophers played Alabama in the Music City Bowl, where Cupito, despite having his mobility limited by a significant

Bryan Cupito, a three-year starter, became the school's all-time leader in career passing yards in 2006.

knee injury, led the Gophers to a 20-16 victory over the Crimson Tide.

Cupito was praised by his teammates and the coaching staff for playing well despite the injury.

"I played hurt, but I don't think it's a big deal," said Cupito. "I've always thought if you can play, you should. It was a little knee injury. I was expected to play. It was blown out of proportion."

The Gophers opened the 2005 season with three victories before playing host to No. 11 Purdue at the Metrodome. In that game, Cupito threw three interceptions—the third was returned for a touchdown, which gave Purdue an eight-point lead with 5:45 remaining. But Cupito and the Gophers showed their resilience as they tied the game to force overtime before winning the game in the second overtime.

He suffered a shoulder injury in the Gophers' 23-20 victory over Michigan and sat out the next week. He returned to the lineup to pass for a career-high 396 yards in the Gophers' loss to Ohio State.

On the season, he passed for 2,530 yards and 19 touchdowns. He completed 59 percent of his passes while throwing just nine interceptions.

SETTING

The Gophers went into the 2006 season with several big holes to fill on offense, and the voids put the focus of the Gophers offense on Cupito, a fifth-year senior.

Gone from 2005 were three players who had moved on to the NFL: running back Laurence Maroney, who had rushed for 3,933 yards in the previous three seasons to become the second-leading rusher in school history; center Greg Eslinger, a three-time All-Big Ten and two-time All-America selection who won the Outland Trophy in 2005 and two-time All-Big Ten selection Mark Setterstrom.

The Gophers, who had five 1,000-yard rushers in the previous three seasons, were expected to rely on Cupito's leadership while throwing the ball more in 2006.

"You can just see that he has put the team on his shoulders and made it his team," Gophers offensive lineman Tony Brinkhaus told the *Minneapolis Star Tribune*. "Knowing him as well as I do, he seems like a completely different person now. Everybody on this team has noticed this new leadership role he's taken."

The Gophers opened the season with a pair of easy victories—44-0 over Kent State and 62-0 over Temple—sandwiched around a 42-17 loss to No. 22 California in Berkeley, California.

On September 23, the Gophers suffered a 27-21 loss at Purdue. The loss began a four-game losing streak, which would put a trip to a fifth-consecutive bowl game in jeopardy. The Gophers scored first, but Purdue scored 20 consecutive points to take a 20-7 lead. Cupito threw two touchdown passes in the second half, but the Boilermakers held on for the victory.

The following week, the Gophers played host to No. 6 Michigan. Cupito passed for 215 yards and two touchdowns as the Gophers played the Wolverines tough, but Michigan prevailed, 28-14.

The slump continued as the Gophers played host to Penn State. After scoring with a minute remaining in regulation to tie the game and scoring first in overtime, the Gophers lost by one point on a missed extra point. Cupito had been nearly flawless as he completed 25 of 36 passes for 347 yards and two touchdowns.

The Gophers next traveled to Madison, Wisconsin, where the No. 25 Badgers built a 41-3 lead in a dominating 48-12 victory over the Gophers. The Badgers outgained the Gophers, 401-200.

The losing streak ended when the Gophers held on for a 10-9 victory over North Dakota State by blocking a 42-yard field goal attempt on the final play of the game. A Metrodome crowd of 62,845 saw the teams play for the first time since 1937.

A 44-0 loss to No. 1 Ohio State the following week left the Gophers with a 3-6 record with three games remaining.

The Gophers regrouped to trounce Indiana, 63-26, on homecoming. The 63 points were the most scored by the Gophers in a Big Ten game in 90 years. Cupito threw three touchdown passes in the first half as the Gophers raced to a 35-7 halftime lead. For the day, Cupito passed for 378 yards and four touchdowns.

The Gophers then improved to 5-6 on the season with a 31-18 victory over Michigan State in East Lansing, Michigan.

Up next for the Gophers were the Iowa Hawkeyes. The Hawkeyes brought a 6-5 record into the game, but had lost four consecutive Big Ten games to fall to 2-5 in the conference.

GAME OF MY LIFE

BY BRYAN CUPITO

It had been a little bit of an up-and-down season. It had been real disappointing. I thought we had more talent than a 5-6 team.

But we had some tough losses—we lost to Purdue by a touchdown. We lost to Penn State by one point in overtime. We lost to Michigan. They beat us by two touchdowns, but we had some opportunities and were in the game.

And we got blown out by Wisconsin, Ohio State, and California. It was a matter of which team showed up for us.

In the middle of the season, we beat North Dakota State by one, when we probably should have lost that game. The next week we got beat by Ohio State and were 3-6 with three games left. And we had to win all three of our remaining games to become bowl eligible.

Going into the Iowa game, we knew if we lost that game our season was over. But when we were 3-6, we knew if we lost any of our last three games our season was over. We had played great in beating Indiana and Michigan State.

Iowa was a huge game. Especially for us seniors—we hadn't beaten them since I'd been at the University. We had no doubt that we could beat them if we played well.

The week leading up to the game, the coaching staff was real positive and came up with a great game plan for us.

It was great to have (tight end) Matt Spaeth available. He's the best player on our team. He was playing with a separated shoulder. I had talked to him right after he hurt it (in the victory over North

Dakota State). He said he could have surgery right away so he'd be healed for the NFL draft combine, or he could play with it and have the surgery after the season, which would mean he wouldn't be ready for the combine. We would have completely understood if he had made the decision to have the surgery right away. But he chose to play, and with him in the lineup, we won our last three games.

To tell you the truth, I had no doubt we were going to win. I didn't think it was going to be our last game. We had a great game plan and were playing at home, where we had played well all season.

It was great. I had a bunch of family and friends from Cincinnati who were at the game. It was great they all could be up for the game.

We just came out and threw the ball and that was working. Then we ran the ball and that worked. We had some real good game plans the last three weeks (of the regular season), mixing it up, and we finally executed real well.

I thought our defense played well and made a couple of huge plays. Mike Sherels made a big interception right before halftime that was huge.

It was a great way to end the season. We had put ourselves in a bad position during the season, but luckily we pulled out a win to make it to a bowl game. It was just one of those games where things went right.

It was great to see the pig (Floyd of Rosedale) up close for the first time. And my daughter really enjoyed it because she got to go on the field.

GAME RESULTS

Faced with their third consecutive must-win game, the Gophers defeated Iowa, 34-24, before 64,140 at the Metrodome. The victory evened the Gophers' record at 6-6 and made them bowl eligible for the seventh time in eight seasons.

The Gophers overcame being outgained by the Hawkeyes, 546-459, by forcing five Hawkeyes turnovers. The Gophers turned the ball over just once and Cupito was solid—completing 18 of 30 passes for 267 yards and two touchdowns.

The Gophers scored on their first possession—on the first of two touchdowns by Amir Pinnix—to take a 6-0 lead in the game's first five minutes, but the Hawkeyes scored late in the first quarter to take a 7-6 lead.

The second quarter was entertaining as each team scored twice.

The Gophers went up 13-7 after a two-yard touchdown run by freshman Jay Thomas. The Hawkeyes immediately responded with an 80-yard scoring drive to regain the lead, 14-13.

On the fourth play after the ensuing kickoff, Cupito connected with Ernie Wheelwright on a 64-yard touchdown pass. The extra-point kick gave the Gophers a 20-14 lead. The Hawkeyes pulled within three, 20-17, with a 37-yard field goal with four minutes remaining in the first half and appeared headed for the go-ahead touchdown right before halftime, but Gophers linebacker Mike Sherels intercepted a pass at the goal line with 31 seconds remaining in the half.

The Gophers scored two touchdowns in a eight-minute span bridging the third and fourth quarters to open a 34-17 lead with 12 minutes remaining. The first touchdown was a three-yard pass from Cupito to Matt Spaeth, who was playing with a shoulder injury that needed surgery.

Pinnix scored his second touchdown—on a 25-yard run—to make it 33-17. Pinnix finished with 119 yards rushing in 23 carries.

The Hawkeyes scored with eight minutes remaining to pull within 10, but couldn't get any closer. They put together a late threat—reaching the Gophers' 25-yard line with 4:12 remaining, but the Gophers stopped them on fourth down.

In his postgame press conference, Gophers coach Glen Mason said, "I am extremely proud of the kids because things haven't exactly gone their way this year. For them to continually to go out after having setbacks and do what they have done is a credit to those kids. They deserve all the credit."

The Gophers accepted a bid to the Insight Bowl in Tempe, Arizona. The Gophers' season ended on a sour note with a 44-41 overtime loss to Texas Tech on December 29. The Red Raiders rallied from a 38-7 deficit early in the third quarter. In his final game, Cupito completed 19 of 31 passes for 263 yards and three touchdowns.

Cupito finished the season with the best single-season marks in school history in several categories: completions (214), yards (2,819), and touchdowns (22).

Two days after the loss to Texas Tech, the University announced that Mason would not return as the Gophers coach.

WHAT HAPPENED TO BRYAN CUPITO?

Cupito finished his Gophers career as the school's all-time leader in career passing yardage (7,446) and tied for first (with Asad Abdul-Khaliq) in career touchdown passes (55). Cupito was second in career completions (513) and attempts (918).

"I had some great players around me, and we've had great running backs and great tight ends and receivers in the system since I've been here," said Cupito. "It's a lot easier to make plays with guys like that around you."

Mason told the media after the Iowa game, "Bryan Cupito has had an outstanding career here. The last couple of years he has been overshadowed by the running game, but we were never one-dimensional. All of a sudden it was announced that he was the passing leader in Minnesota history, and I thought it was fitting today how he ended his regular-season career."

Cupito, who majored in business and marketing education, earned his undergraduate degree in four years. Cupito played his senior season while pursuing a master's degree in sports management.

Cupito, who interned with a sports marketing company in early 2007, said his playing days were likely over. After not being invited to the NFL scouting combine (28 quarterbacks were invited), Cupito decided not to pursue a free agent tryout with an NFL team.

Cupito, the father of a one-year old daughter, did not rule out a job in coaching while he pursued a job in the business world upon completion of his graduate degree.

Chapter 21

ED
LECHNER

EARLY LIFE OF ED LECHNER

Lechner, the youngest of three children, grew up on a farm in North Dakota. Lechner attended a one-room schoolhouse through the eighth grade. Many of the farm children of the era did not go to school past the eighth grade.

"Some of the neighbors told my dad that he was wasting his time sending his children to high school," said Lechner. "But my parents encouraged me to get an education."

In the fall of 1933, Lechner began attending Fessenden High school. Farm life hadn't left much time for extra-curricular activities or diversions.

Prior to his sophomore year of high school, Lechner had never seen a football game. But as a sophomore, he was asked to go out for the Fessenden High School team. Lechner, who joined 17 other boys on the squad, was a quick study at football.

As a junior he earned all-conference honors as Fessenden lost just one game and won a conference title. As a senior, Lechner earned all-state honors as he helped Fessenden go unbeaten, without surrendering a single score (outscoring their opponents, 105-0).

After graduation, Lechner's intention was to go to the University of North Dakota and study medicine. But his plans changed after a trip to Minneapolis in the summer of 1937. Lechner's trip was for his brother Lawrence's wedding. While in Minneapolis, Lawrence took his younger brother on a visit to the University of Minnesota. While on campus, Lawrence introduced Ed to Gopher football coach Bernie Bierman.

NAME: Ed Lechner
BORN: December 14, 1919
HOMETOWN: Fessenden, North Dakota
POSITION: Tackle
HEIGHT: 6-1
WEIGHT: 210
YEARS: 1939-1941, 1943
ACCOMPLISHMENTS: Played in 1941 Blue-Gray Classic.
GAME: vs. Northwestern—November 1, 1941

"Lawrence told Bierman that I could play football," said Lechner. "Bierman was impressed that I had also run track and thought that I might make a good end."

After initially trying out as an end, Lechner was undecided if he should continue to pursue football. But in his sophomore year he moved up to third team on the depth chart. Lechner got his first significant playing time against Michigan and Tom Harmon after starter Sy Johnson suffered a dislocated elbow the previous week against Northwestern.

In 1940, the Gophers had talented linemen like Dick Wildung and Urban Odson. Lechner proved to be a valuable backup.

"Bernie [Bierman] always rotated players," said Lechner. "He liked to rotate at least two guys at every position. He liked the depth. He liked to wear opponents down with fresh players."

In 1941, because of injuries, Lechner played regularly—starting two games at left tackle and four games at right tackle.

SETTING

The Gophers, who had won the national title in 1940, were ranked No. 1 in the 1941 Associated Press preseason poll.

The Gophers opened the 1941 season on September 27 in Seattle with a 14-6 victory over Washington. The Gophers returned home and improved to 3-0, with impressive victories over Illinois (34-6) and Pittsburgh (39-0).

On Oct. 25, the Gophers passed a big test with a 7-0 victory over No. 3 Michigan before 85,000 in Ann Arbor, Michigan. But the victory over the Wolverines came with a price—halfbacks Bruce Smith and Herman Frickey, who had scored the Gophers' touchdown, were injured. Two other key players—Odson, a tackle, and guard Helge Pukema, who both had earned All-American honors in 1940—were also injured going into the Northwestern game.

Northwestern, which was looking to avenge a heartbreaking 13-12 loss to the Gophers in 1940, brought a 3-1 record into the game. The Wildcats had opened the season with easy victories over Kansas State (51-3) and Wisconsin (41-14) before losing to Michigan (14-7). The Wildcats rebounded to defeat Ohio State, 14-7, in Columbus, Ohio.

The Wildcats went into the game in Minneapolis healthier than the Gophers, although tackle Tony Samatzia was sidelined and star halfback Otto Graham was playing with a fractured nose.

Headlines in the Minneapolis newspapers said "Injuries lessen Gopher chances" and "Crippled Gophers no better than even choice."

GAME OF MY LIFE

BY ED LECHNER

I don't know why, but I always played my best against Northwestern. Against Northwestern in 1940, Bill DeCoorevont looked like he was going to score a touchdown. I was playing end on the opposite side and I was able to catch him from behind. Bernie couldn't believe that I caught him.

The previous week we had played Michigan. Before that game Bernie thought Michigan was going to be the toughest of the next two games. And he thought we needed something extra because Bruce Smith was out and we were banged up a little.

So we practiced a trick play that Bernie had seen at the East-West Shrine game the previous year. We never showed the play to anyone. But against Michigan we were leading and never had to use it.

Against Northwestern we got a safety early in the game. But Northwestern got a touchdown in the second quarter on a pass from Otto

The 1941 Gophers were named the national champions—marking the fifth time for the Gophers in eight seasons. Ed Lechner (#86) is second from the right in the first row.

Graham and we trailed 7-2 at halftime. Late in the third quarter we were still trailing, 7-2, and people were starting to get a little nervous.

We held and the Wildcats lined up to punt from their own 15-yard line. Northwestern's punter had been a little slow kicking the ball and in the first quarter we had come close to blocking a kick. I was at right tackle and they left me open. All I had to do was shoot straight through and I was able to get a piece of the ball. The ball went out of bounds at the 41. If we hadn't blocked it, we would have gotten the ball at our own 20- or 30-yard line and it would have been tough.

Bernie had told the officials before the game about our trick play. They were nice enough not to spill it. The situation had to be just right to use the play. It was a once-in-a-season type of play.

After the punt, Bernie sent Urban Odson in with the instructions for the play. And I went to the sideline. We were going to use it on our second play. Bob Swieger ran out of bounds on our first play and he was supposed to argue a little after the play. He got hit pretty good by a couple of Wildcats and he started arguing with them about piling on.

Our line was kind of standing around talking. We didn't go into a huddle. Northwestern was waiting for us to go into a huddle. When the referee put the ball down, our center Gene Flick flipped the ball to Higgins, who took off. He got behind Odson and went into for a touchdown.

The play went so fast, that our photographer, Phil Brain, missed the start of it. The Chicago newspapers said the play was illegal.

It was a miracle the play went off without a hitch. It was a thrill to see Higgins score. After we scored, we had such a good defense, we were able to shut Northwestern down the rest of the game.

The whole season was a miracle. We had a different backfield every game because of injuries.

GAME RESULTS

In the *Minneapolis Sunday Tribune* the next day, Charles Johnson credited Lechner for "playing a great game" and blocking DeCoorevont's kick to set up the trick play.

Johnson, whose newspaper career spanned more than 50 years, wrote that the trick play was the "most deceptive ever pulled in Minnesota's football history. [It] will create more talk than anything that has happened in football this year or many years in the past. If the record crowd [64,464] would tell the truth, 99 percent of them would admit that they never saw what took place."

The *Chicago Tribune*'s account of the game was headlined, "Gophers score 14th straight on trick play."

Despite the 8-7 victory over Northwestern, the Gophers dropped to No. 2 in the Associated Press poll. No. 2 Texas moved into the No. 1 spot after a 34-0 victory over No. 20 SMU. The Gophers returned to the No. 1 spot one week later after they defeated Nebraska, 9-0, and Texas played to a 7-7 tie with unranked Baylor.

On Nov. 15, the return of Bruce Smith, who had missed parts of five games because of injuries, sparked the Gophers to a 34-13 victory over Iowa in Iowa City. The Gophers closed out their second consecutive unbeaten season with a 41-6 victory over Wisconsin. Following the season, the Gophers were named the national champion—their fifth national title since 1934—and Smith was awarded the Heisman Trophy.

Lechner played in the Blue-Gray Classic in Montgomery, Alabama. The North team was coached by Northwestern coach Pappy Waldorf. On Dec. 27, the South defeated the North, 16-0, before 15,000 fans.

"I became friends with Waldorf," said Lechner. "He told me, 'Ed, you were a thorn in our side.'"

WHAT HAPPENED TO ED LECHNER?

In the spring of 1942, Dr. George Hauser became the Gophers coach after Bernie Bierman, who had entered military service. Hauser asked Lechner to help coach spring practice.

That summer, Jack Mara, the president of the NFL New York Giants, offered a contract and Lechner joined the Giants in Superior, Wisconsin, for training camp. Lechner appeared in four games with the Giants, who were coached by future Pro Football Hall of Fame coach Steve Owen. The Giants opened their season with a 14-7 victory over the Washington Redskins in Washington. The loss was the only one of the season for the Redskins, who went 10-1 and won the NFL title.

Following his time with the Giants, he returned to Minneapolis to continue his dental studies. In the spring of 1943, he was again asked by Hauser to help coach the Gophers. Because of war-time eligibility rules, Lechner was eligible to play for the Gophers in 1943. He appeared in the Gophers' first three games before suffering a knee injury against Camp Grant.

After graduating from dental school in 1944, Lechner served in the U.S. Navy. Lechner served abroad the U.S.S. Vicksburg in the Pacific before being discharged in November of 1946. He returned to Minnesota and eventually opened a practice in the Highland Park neighborhood of St. Paul.

In the early 1960s, he became the team dentist for the Minnesota Vikings of the NFL. He held that position for 20 years. He also served as president of the Minnesota State Dental Board and practiced dentistry into his 80s.

In early 2013, Lechner was living in a retirement village in Minnesota and was listed as the 23rd oldest living former professional football player/contributor, according to a pro football website.

Chapter 22

ERIC DECKER

EARLY LIFE OF ERIC DECKER

Eric Decker's father Tom Decker played college football and basketball. His sister Sarah was a high school state track champion and competed in track in college.

So it wasn't a surprise that Eric Decker was an athletic standout in high school. But his high school football coach said something besides genetics made Decker successful.

"Eric's got the right gene pool," Rick Theisen told the *St. Cloud Times*, "There's athleticism in his family, but his mindset has a lot to do with it too. With Eric, you never heard 'good enough.' He was always working harder than anyone on our team—and he didn't have to work that hard because he was good enough to get by on talent alone."

Decker's talent helped him earn all-area honors from the *St. Cloud Times* in three sports—football, basketball and baseball.

"I never thought about [specializing or concentrating on] one sport. I enjoyed the variety," said Decker. "I think it's important for kids to have variety and have a break so they don't get burned out.

"I think playing all three sports helped me become a better athlete. The hand-eye coordination needed for baseball helped me in football, catching the ball. The agility needed in basketball helped me be a better receiver."

NAME: Eric Decker
BORN: March 15, 1987
HOMETOWN: Cold Spring, Minnesota
POSITION: Wide receiver
HEIGHT: 6-3
WEIGHT: 218
YEARS: 2006-2009
ACCOMPLISHMENTS: First team All-Big Ten in 2008 and 2009; Bronko Nagurski Award (Team MVP) in 2009; Bruce Smith Award (Team outstanding offensive performer) in 2007, 2008 (shared with Adam Weber) and 2009.
GAME: vs. Air Force, September 12, 2009

As a senior at Rocori High School, Decker caught 62 passes for 1,017 yards and 15 touchdowns to earn all-state and all-Midwest honors. A three-year starter in football, Decker finished his career with 2,156 receiving yards and 28 touchdowns.

Decker also succeeded in the classroom. Decker, a member of the National Honor Society, earned Academic All-State honors. Prior to the start of his senior year, Decker was offered a football scholarship by Gophers coach Glen Mason. Decker, who had been recruited by many Division I schools, accepted.

"I wasn't a guy who went to a lot of camps in the summer," said Decker. "I played in a basketball league and amateur baseball in the summer. I went to a one-day camp at Minnesota and they offered me a scholarship. If I hadn't gone to the U, I would have gone to St. John's [in nearby Collegeville, MN]."

SETTING

After redshirting in 2005, Decker started three games for the Gophers in 2006. He caught 26 passes and scored three touchdowns for the Gophers, who went 6-6 in the regular season before losing to Texas Tech in overtime in the Insight Bowl.

Decker became a full-time starter as a sophomore in 2007. He led the Gophers with 67 receptions for 909 yards and nine touchdowns.

Despite missing most of two games in 2008 because of a high ankle sprain, Decker set a school record with 84 receptions. His 1,074 receiving yards were the second-most in school history. In a 16-7 victory over

Indiana on Oct. 4, he had 13 receptions (tying the school single-game record set by Aaron Osterman against Michigan in 1994) for 190 yards (third-best in school history). Following the season he was named first-team All-Big Ten.

The Gophers opened the 2009 season with a 23-20 overtime victory at Syracuse. After catching just two passes for 50 yards in the first three quarters, Decker finished with nine receptions for 183 yards. His 38-yard reception set up the Gophers' second touchdown and his receptions set up the Gophers' game-tying and game-winning field goals.

The season-opening victory gave the Gophers momentum heading into their home-opener (in the first football stadium constructed in the Big Ten Conference since 1960).

GAME OF MY LIFE

BY ERIC DECKER

Going into the 2009 season, we were real excited about our offensive firepower. We started the season with the victory over Syracuse and we were excited going into the first game at TCF Bank Stadium.

It was very exciting to be a part of the first class to open up the stadium. It was a special day. It's what college football is all about—getting the students and the entire campus involved; the camaraderie; the home field advantage.

Playing Air Force, with their ball-control offense, we knew we wouldn't have that many [offensive] possessions. We didn't move the ball well early in the game.

We were trailing 10-3 going into the fourth quarter and then we tied the score after a long drive early in the fourth quarter. Then on Air Force's next possession, Nate Triplett scooped up a fumble [forced by the Gophers' Brandon Kirksey] and went 52 yards for the [go-ahead] touchdown. It was awesome, the place was crowded and packed [a sell-out crowd of 50,805].

I think the entire day was special, but three moments really stand out. One was the fly-over by jets before the game. Then, coming out the tunnel onto the field for the first time. And Nate Triplett scooping up the fumble.

GAME RESULTS

Decker's 10 receptions for 113 yards helped the Gophers rally for an emotional 20-13 victory over the Falcons in the first-ever meeting between the two programs.

After the game, Decker told reporters, "I think after the first drive we settled down. I think the emotion was still running [during] the first kickoff and the first drive, but after that we realized it was just another ball game but a special one, at home with the crowd and everything. And you know, the first half we struggled a little bit but came back the second half and got things rolling and made some plays.

"I think we just got more confident with ourselves and we started making plays, executing our offense. You know getting the third-and-short, converting first downs. We finally were moving the ball and the first half we kind of shot ourselves in the foot a little bit with some penalties. I know myself, I had three penalties this game. It's those little things that add up. I think we did a better job of eliminating them.

"You know, we came out slow the last two games and that's something we need to work on. I mean, obviously in practice we will try to work on those things and try to get the ball rolling right away. But it's good to see that we don't give up."

The following week, the Gophers lost at No. 8 California, 35-21. In week 4, Decker caught two touchdown passes in the Gophers' 35-24 victory at Northwestern.

Decker's season came to an end when he suffered a foot injury in the Gophers' 38-7 loss at No. 18 Ohio State on Oct. 18. The injury—a torn ligament and torn tendon—required surgery.

Despite missing the Gophers' final four regular season games and bowl

---

Eric Decker led the Gophers in receiving in three consecutive seasons and holds school records for receptions and receiving yards.

game (a 14-13 loss to Iowa State in the Insight Bowl), Decker led the Gophers with 50 receptions for 785 yards and five touchdowns. Despite missing three conference games, he was named first-team All-Big Ten.

Decker finished his Gophers career with school records for receptions (227) and receiving yards (3,119). His 24 touchdown receptions are third-most—behind Ron Johnson (31) and Ernie Wheelwright (26)—in school history. He caught a pass in 34 consecutive games—the second-best streak in school history behind Ron Johnson's 45-game streak (which is a Big Ten record).

Decker, who had 11 games with more than 100 receiving yards in his Gophers career, dropped only three passes in his four-year career.

WHAT HAPPENED TO ERIC DECKER?

Decker was a two-sport star and academic standout for the Gophers. A three-time Academic All-Big Ten selection, Decker graduated with a degree in Business Marketing Education in 3½ years. During his final season with the Gophers football team, he took two graduate classes in Sports Management.

During his Minnesota career, he spent two seasons with the Gophers baseball team. He hit .329 for the Gophers in 2008. In June of 2008 he was selected by the Milwaukee Brewers in the 39th round of Major League Baseball's Amateur Draft. In 2009, he hit .319 for the Gophers. Following that season he was selected by the Minnesota Twins in the 27th round of the Amateur Draft.

In April of 2010, Decker was selected by the Denver Broncos in the third round of the NFL draft. Decker signed a four-year contract with the Broncos.

After a successful preseason—he led all NFL players with 16 receptions in the preseason—he appeared in 14 regular season games as a rookie. He led the Broncos in kick returns (22 for 556 yards) and caught six passes for 106 yards. He caught a 6-yard pass from Tim Tebow in the Broncos' regular season finale for his first career touchdown.

In 2011, Decker led the Broncos with 44 receptions. His eight receiving touchdowns were the second-most by a Denver player in his first or second year. In his first game returning punts—at any level—he returned a punt 90 yards for a touchdown against the Oakland Raiders. It was the third-longest punt return in team history.

Also in 2011, Decker was named to the USA Football All-Fundamentals team.

In his third season, Decker blossomed into one of the top receivers in the NFL. He had 85 receptions for 1,064 yards. His 13 receiving touchdowns were second-most in the NFL (Green Bay's James Jones caught 14 touchdown passes) and set a Denver team record for receiving touchdowns in a two-season span (21).

He caught at least seven passes in six games and caught two touchdown passes in a game on four occasions. Decker and teammate Demaryius Thomas combined for 23 receiving touchdowns (the most by any duo in the NFL) and 2,498 receiving yards (third-most in the league).

"Right now, I see a big body, a big athlete, a good football player, a smart football player who understands what [Broncos quarterback] Peyton [Manning] is looking for, what he's looking at," Carolina Panthers coach Ron Rivera told *The Denver Post* at midseason in 2012. "I think any time you have that rapport with a quarterback and a receiver, you can have that success."

Decker and Manning started working out together soon after the four-time NFL MVP signed with the Broncos in March of 2012.

Decker told *The Denver Post* during the 2012 season, "I think, obviously, all the work you do—individually, extra, as a team—has paid off. Peyton grabs everybody, and we all work on it together. That's something that's finally paying off. I think any relationship, whether it's a significant other or a teammate, the more time it gets, it helps."

Decker said, "I've been fortunate. I'm with a great organization in a great city."